NGOs and Global Civil Society

NGOs and Global Civil Society

Dong-uk Kim

PNUPRESS

Table of Contents

Chapter 1. Introduction

In the twenty-first century, our daily lives are shaped by forces and connections that transcend national borders. The goods we buy, the information we share, the climate we depend on, and the human rights we claim—none of these can be fully understood or protected within the boundaries of a single country. Yet even as states negotiate treaties and multinational corporations expand their reach, there is a third actor whose presence is equally critical but often less understood: civil society.

This book, NGOs and Global Civil Society, is designed to help students, practitioners, and emerging leaders grasp why civil society matters in a world defined by globalization and governance challenges that no government or market can solve alone. At its heart lies a simple but powerful premise: when people organize voluntarily, they can transform societies, shift norms, and hold even the most powerful institutions to account.

From the anti-slavery movements of the nineteenth century to modern environmental campaigns, human rights struggles, and digital activism, civil society has played a decisive role in expanding freedoms and creating spaces for democratic dialogue. NGOs (nongovernmental organizations) and community-based organizations (CBOs) have become central to this story. They lobby for new laws, deliver essential services where states fall short, expose corruption and injustice, and build bridges across cultures and borders.

However, this influence is neither automatic nor uncontested. Civil society does not exist in a vacuum; it is embedded in complex webs of power, resources, technology, and politics. Over the past decades, NGOs have professionalized, scaled up, and globalized—securing consultative status at the United Nations, partnering with corporations to promote Corporate Social Responsibility (CSR), and shaping global development agendas like the Sustainable Development Goals (SDGs). But this growth has brought new questions: Who speaks for whom? Who funds civil society—and on what terms? How do NGOs balance local legitimacy with global reach? How can they stay true to their mission while navigating partnerships with states and multinational corporations whose interests may not always align with those of the communities they serve?

This book invites you to examine these questions critically and constructively. It begins by exploring how globalization has redefined political and economic life since World War II, tracing the rise of institutions such as the International Monetary Fund (IMF) and the World Trade Organization (WTO) that set the rules of global engagement. It then situates civil society within this system, showing how grassroots actors have responded to, shaped, and sometimes resisted the flows of capital, ideas, and power.

We look at the historical evolution of NGOs—from the pioneering work of abolitionists and the birth of the International Committee of the Red Cross, to the proliferation of humanitarian aid and human rights networks in the aftermath of world wars and during the Cold War. We examine how digital technologies have transformed civic organizing, enabling transnational campaigns and real-time solidarity—but also giving rise to new forms of surveillance, disinformation, and censorship that threaten freedom of expression and democratic space.

You will encounter key debates that animate the field today: How should NGOs relate to states? What role should they play in delivering public goods when governments fail? Should they collaborate with corporations through cross-sector partnerships, or does this risk co-optation and mission drift? How can civil society defend civic space and digital rights in an age of algorithmic governance and surveillance capitalism?

Throughout these chapters, you will see that NGOs and global civil society are not static categories. They are dynamic, diverse, and sometimes contradictory. They include large international charities with multi-million-dollar budgets and neighborhood mutual aid groups run by volunteers. They include faith-based networks, environmental coalitions, feminist movements, Indigenous rights campaigns, youth climate strikers, and digital rights defenders. Their tactics range from direct service delivery to lobbying, litigation, mass mobilization, and online advocacy.

This diversity is both a strength and a challenge. It means civil society can adapt and innovate in the face of crises—whether responding to pandemics, mobilizing around climate justice, or resisting authoritarian crackdowns. But it also means civil society is vulnerable to fragmentation, internal inequality, and external pressures that can weaken its transformative potential.

The final chapters of this book look forward. They ask what new forms of funding, leadership, partnership, and technological literacy are needed to ensure that NGOs and CBOs remain resilient and relevant. They emphasize the importance of trust-based philanthropy, participatory governance, intergenerational leadership, and the "invisible infrastructure" of good governance, secure digital systems, and local accountability that keep civil society strong from within.

Above all, this book challenges you to see yourself as part of this story. Whether you aspire to work in an NGO, shape policy, or simply be an engaged citizen, you have a stake in how civil society evolves. The debates in these pages are not abstract—they are about the real struggles that will define your generation: climate change, forced migration, global inequality, digital surveillance, democratic backsliding, and the search for new models of solidarity that transcend borders and divisions.

By the end of your journey through these chapters, you will have the tools to analyze how global civil society functions, how it negotiates power, and how it can hold markets and states accountable. More importantly, you will be equipped to ask the next questions: What does it mean to be a global citizen? How can you contribute to strengthening civic space in your own community? And how might you help imagine, build, and defend a more just, peaceful, and sustainable global future?

Welcome to the study of NGOs and Global Civil Society.

Your questions—and your actions—start here.

Learning Objectives

By the end of this chapter, students will be able to:

- Define globalization and explain its political, economic, and technological dimensions.
- Describe how political institutions influence global economic relations.
- Analyze the historical development of global governance since World War II.
- Evaluate the roles of state and non-state actors in shaping the global economy.
- Identify key tensions and challenges in achieving equitable global governance.

The Political Origins of Globalization and the Post-War World Order

Since the end of the Second World War, the modern global economy has never existed in isolation from political decisions, institutions, and the competing visions of how societies should be organized. While markets and economic theories are often portrayed as driven by universal laws of supply and demand, the true story of globalization is far more complex and deeply political. Behind the flows of capital, goods, services, and ideas lie power struggles, shifting alliances, and ideological contests that have shaped how nations trade, invest, cooperate, and compete for influence.

In the decades following 1945, the idea of globalization came to signify not just the expansion of economic activity beyond national borders but also the interdependence of societies in ways that defy simple economic models. It is about who sets the rules of engagement, who benefits from the outcomes, and who bears the costs. This process has been marked by moments of optimism, crisis, realignment, and resistance—each leaving an imprint on the global order we know today.

In the immediate post-war years, leaders and economists recognized that unchecked economic rivalry could again lead to devastating conflicts like those that had ravaged Europe twice in half a century. To prevent this, the United States and its allies convened a new system of international economic institutions designed to stabilize currencies, rebuild economies, and foster cooperation. The 1944 Bretton Woods Conference established the International Monetary Fund (IMF) and the World Bank. Their mission was clear: to provide financial assistance and oversight to prevent currency collapses, balance-of-payment crises, and beggar-thy-neighbor policies that had destabilized the interwar period.

These institutions reflected the Western liberal vision that freer trade and open markets would tie countries together in mutual prosperity and peace. The General

Agreement on Tariffs and Trade (GATT), signed in 1947, further codified this vision by promoting tariff reductions and multilateral trade negotiations. The logic was that economic interdependence would reduce the incentives for conflict—a powerful idea that has shaped decades of international policy.

The Cold War and the Politics of Development in the Global South

Yet the world did not neatly converge on this liberal economic order. The Cold War quickly divided the globe into two opposing camps. In the Western bloc, the Marshall Plan poured billions of dollars into rebuilding Europe, binding the continent's economic recovery to the United States and its market-oriented model. In the Eastern bloc, the Soviet Union and its allies pursued centralized planning and state ownership, building an alternative system of economic governance that rejected capitalist principles. This ideological rivalry shaped trade routes, aid flows, and the politics of development far beyond Europe.

The impact of this division was most visible in the so-called Third World—nations in Asia, Africa, and Latin America emerging from centuries of colonial domination. These newly independent states often found themselves battlegrounds for Cold War influence. Both the U.S. and the USSR used economic tools—development aid, investment, trade preferences, and military support—to secure allies and contain the other's expansion. For many countries, economic choices were inseparable from security calculations and ideological alignment.

By the early 1970s, however, the stability of the Bretton Woods system came under strain. The United States, grappling with inflation, trade deficits, and the costs of the Vietnam War, abandoned the gold standard in 1971, ending the dollar's convertibility to gold. This decision unleashed floating exchange rates, introducing new volatility into global finance. At the same time, the 1973 oil crisis—triggered by the OPEC oil embargo—exposed the West's vulnerability to resource shocks and fueled a new era of economic interdependence.

In response, developing countries, many rich in oil and raw materials, sought to renegotiate their place in the global economy. The call for a New International Economic Order (NIEO) in the 1970s reflected demands for fairer trade terms, technology transfers, and greater representation in global institutions. While the NIEO ultimately fell short of its transformative goals, it signaled a growing awareness that the benefits of globalization were unequally distributed.

Systemic Transitions and the Technological Acceleration of Globalization

The end of the Cold War in 1989 marked another turning point. The collapse of the Soviet Union removed a major ideological competitor to liberal capitalism. Countries in Eastern Europe and the former Soviet republics embarked on ambitious programs of privatization, market liberalization, and political democratization—often with significant support and conditionality from the IMF and World Bank. Yet this transition was far from smooth. In Russia, for instance, the rapid privatization of state assets created powerful oligarchs and deepened inequalities, undermining public trust in democratic reforms.

China's trajectory offered a striking counterpoint. Beginning with Deng Xiaoping's economic reforms in the late 1970s, China opened its markets to foreign investment and global trade while maintaining strict political control. This "socialist market economy" defied conventional Western assumptions that economic liberalization would inevitably lead to political democratization. Instead, China's hybrid model propelled it to become a central actor in the global economy while retaining an authoritarian governance system—a reality that continues to challenge Western policy frameworks.

Meanwhile, technological advancements accelerated globalization to levels unimaginable in previous eras. Container shipping, the rise of just-in-time manufacturing, and revolutionary improvements in information and communications technologies (ICTs) drastically reduced the cost and time needed to move goods, services, money, and ideas across borders. The internet in particular transformed how companies operate, how supply chains are organized, and how consumers engage with markets. Financial markets became hyper-connected, enabling instant capital flows but also exposing economies to new forms of systemic risk.

Yet technological progress also deepened divisions. The "digital divide" between those with reliable access to digital tools and those without reinforced old inequalities and created new ones. Advanced economies and tech-savvy sectors reaped the benefits of the knowledge economy, while workers in traditional industries faced job displacement, wage stagnation, and growing precarity. This tension fueled waves of political backlash against globalization, evident in movements advocating for protectionist policies, national sovereignty, and stricter immigration controls.

Financial Crises, Inequality, and the Globalization Backlash

The 2008 global financial crisis starkly revealed the fragility of the interconnected global economy. What began as a collapse in the U.S. subprime mortgage market rapidly escalated into a worldwide recession, erasing trillions in wealth, bankrupting major institutions, and causing deep social and political fallout. The crisis triggered new debates about financial regulation, the power of multinational banks, and the role of international institutions in crisis management.

In the aftermath, emerging economies—China, India, Brazil, and others—gained greater prominence in global economic forums like the G20, reflecting a more multipolar world order. Yet tensions over trade imbalances, currency manipulation, and the rules of digital commerce remain persistent sources of friction.

Civil Society, the Climate Crisis, and the Reshaping of Global Governance

At the heart of these debates lies the question of global governance: how can diverse states and non-state actors cooperate to manage the opportunities and risks of globalization? Institutions like the WTO, IMF, and World Bank have long provided the rules and mechanisms for negotiation and dispute resolution. Yet they face growing criticism for being dominated by wealthy countries and for failing to adapt to new realities such as climate change, digital trade, and the rise of transnational corporations whose power sometimes rivals that of states.

Civil society actors—NGOs, social movements, and transnational advocacy networks—have emerged as critical voices demanding greater transparency, accountability, and inclusivity in global decision-making. They have shaped debates on human rights, labor standards, environmental protection, and data privacy. For example, campaigns to link trade agreements with climate commitments reflect a broader recognition that economic policies cannot be separated from ecological and social sustainability.

The COVID-19 pandemic further underscored the interdependence—and vulnerability—of the global system. Disruptions in supply chains, unequal access to vaccines, and debates over intellectual property rights highlighted the tensions between national interests and global solidarity. Public-private partnerships, global health initiatives, and grassroots organizing demonstrated the importance of cooperation, but also the limits of current governance structures to ensure fair and effective outcomes.

Looking ahead, the future of globalization will depend on how states, international organizations, and civil society adapt to these challenges. Balancing openness with resilience, efficiency with fairness, and growth with sustainability will require new models of cooperation and innovative approaches to governance. The promise of globalization was never simply economic growth—it was that increased interconnectedness could foster peace, prosperity, and shared responsibility. Whether this promise can be renewed will be one of the defining tests of the twenty-first century.

As the twenty-first century advances, new forms of globalization continue to test old assumptions about economic interdependence and political authority. The digital economy, for example, has created entire industries that exist almost entirely in cyberspace. Companies like Google, Amazon, Facebook, and Alibaba connect billions of people and mediate huge flows of information, capital, and commerce. These companies influence elections, shape public debate, and even challenge state power—yet they often operate in regulatory gray zones that outpace the ability of national governments to set effective rules.

The digital realm also intensifies the link between globalization and individual lives. Personal data—once considered private—is now one of the world's most valuable resources, fueling an economy built on targeted advertising, predictive analytics, and algorithmic decision-making. This raises profound questions for global governance: Who owns data? Who protects privacy? How do we balance innovation and economic dynamism with fundamental rights and social justice?

The debate over data sovereignty illustrates how traditional notions of borders and jurisdiction struggle to keep up with new realities. For example, the European Union's General Data Protection Regulation (GDPR) set new standards for data privacy that reach far beyond Europe's borders, affecting any company that processes EU citizens' data. Meanwhile, countries like China have imposed strict data localization laws, requiring that certain types of data stay within national territory. These divergent approaches highlight the challenges of building coherent global frameworks for digital governance.

Trade is another area where globalization's tensions become clear. While free trade agreements have expanded markets and lifted millions out of poverty, they have also sparked local resistance and backlash. The backlash often stems from the perception—sometimes justified, sometimes exploited for political gain—that globalization enriches elites while hollowing out traditional industries and communities. In the United States and Europe, populist movements have leveraged fears about job loss, cultural erosion, and economic insecurity to question open borders and multilateral trade deals.

One striking example was the United Kingdom's Brexit referendum. While economic arguments for remaining in the European Union were strong, the Leave campaign successfully tapped into anxieties about national sovereignty, immigration, and the perceived loss of local control to distant bureaucrats in Brussels. Brexit demonstrated that economic integration can only be sustained if it retains broad public legitimacy—a lesson with implications far beyond Europe.

Meanwhile, the climate crisis has emerged as perhaps the greatest test of global governance yet. Climate change knows no borders, yet its impacts are profoundly unequal. Industrialized nations have historically emitted the bulk of greenhouse gases, while developing countries—particularly small island states and low-lying coastal regions—face some of the gravest consequences. Global efforts like the Paris Agreement aim to coordinate national commitments and hold states accountable for reducing emissions, but implementation gaps, financing challenges, and political resistance persist.

Transnational NGOs and grassroots movements have become crucial in pressuring governments and corporations to act on climate commitments. Youth-led protests, such as the Fridays for Future movement inspired by Greta Thunberg, have mobilized millions to demand a more just and sustainable global economy. Civil society groups also play a vital role in ensuring that climate solutions consider local needs, indigenous rights, and social equity—not just carbon metrics or corporate profit.

Financial globalization is another domain where the benefits and risks are deeply intertwined. Innovations in financial engineering and the liberalization of capital markets have enabled trillions of dollars to move instantly across borders, funding infrastructure, businesses, and innovation. Yet these same flows can cause sudden crises when investor sentiment shifts. The Asian Financial Crisis of 1997–1998 and the Global Financial Crisis of 2008 revealed how quickly local shocks can become global meltdowns when regulatory oversight and coordination fail.

In response, international bodies like the G20 and the Financial Stability Board have tried to strengthen cooperation among central banks, regulators, and financial institutions. New frameworks for banking supervision, macroprudential oversight, and financial transparency have emerged, but challenges remain. Tax havens, opaque ownership structures, and regulatory loopholes allow illicit financial flows, tax evasion, and corporate profit shifting to undermine the fair distribution of globalization's gains.

These issues underscore the growing importance of fair and transparent institutions. Governance structures must be capable of adapting to rapid changes while remaining accountable to the diverse stakeholders they affect. This includes not only states but also cities, regions, private firms, civil society organizations, and, increasingly, ordinary citizens acting through digital platforms.

One of the defining features of contemporary global governance is the proliferation of public-private partnerships. In areas ranging from global health to infrastructure and sustainable development, governments increasingly rely on alliances with corporations and philanthropic foundations. The COVID-19 pandemic offered a vivid example: initiatives like COVAX brought together states, pharmaceutical companies, NGOs, and international organizations to coordinate vaccine access. Yet stark disparities in vaccine distribution revealed deep power imbalances and raised questions about equity and trust.

The evolution of global governance is also influenced by rising multipolarity. The growing influence of China, India, Brazil, and regional organizations like the African Union challenges the dominance of Western-centric institutions established in the mid-twentieth century. Emerging powers demand greater voice and representation, calling for reforms to the UN Security Council, the IMF quota system, and the leadership structures of the World Bank. Whether existing institutions can adapt or whether new parallel frameworks will emerge remains an open question.

Toward Inclusive and Resilient Globalization: Challenges for the Future

Looking ahead, several key principles will shape whether globalization delivers on its promise of inclusive prosperity or fractures into competing blocs. First is the need for fairness—addressing the structural inequalities within and among countries that globalization can deepen if left unchecked. Second is resilience—designing economic systems and supply chains that can withstand shocks, from pandemics to geopolitical tensions to climate disasters. Third is legitimacy—ensuring that the rules of the global economy are not imposed top-down by powerful states or corporations but are co-created through broad, meaningful participation.

Equally important is the role of education in equipping citizens with the knowledge, skills, and civic capacity to engage critically with globalization. Understanding how trade, technology, finance, and governance interconnect empowers people to hold institutions accountable and to imagine alternatives when current systems fail. Civic engagement, journalism, and academic research are vital parts of the infrastructure that sustains a healthy global public sphere.

Ultimately, the story of globalization is not a single story. It is a contest over whose voices count, whose interests shape the rules, and how we navigate our interdependence in a fractured yet connected world. It is about choices—political, economic, ethical—that will determine whether the promise of globalization is fulfilled as a pathway to peace, prosperity, and human flourishing or remains a source of deepening division and conflict.

As the twenty-first century unfolds, the task for global governance is not simply to manage flows of trade and capital but to forge pathways of cooperation that balance economic dynamism with social justice, technological progress with human rights, and global interconnection with respect for local contexts. The stakes could not be higher—for if we fail, the risks are not only economic disruption but profound challenges to democracy, security, and the very fabric of our shared planet.

Related Article to Read:

Garrad, V. (2018, April 14). The Turn of the Screw: The Impact of Globalisation on Global Governance. E-International Relations. Retrieved from https://www.e-ir.info/2018/04/14/the-turn-of-the-screw-the-impact-of-globalisation-on-global-governance

➔ Key Summary

In "The Turn of the Screw: The Impact of Globalisation on Global Governance," Garrad (2018) explores how globalization has deeply transformed the landscape of global governance—creating opportunities for cooperation but also amplifying new tensions and contradictions. The article argues that globalization is not a uniform or linear process but rather a complex web of economic, political, and cultural interactions that affect the power and effectiveness of governance structures at the global level.

Garrad explains that traditional models of governance based on state sovereignty and fixed borders have struggled to keep pace with transnational issues such as climate change, financial crises, migration, and terrorism. While international organizations like the UN, IMF, and WTO attempt to manage these challenges through multilateral cooperation, they often face legitimacy crises, gridlock, and accusations of favoring powerful states or corporate interests.

The piece further highlights how non-state actors—such as NGOs, multinational corporations, and global civil society networks—have become increasingly influential in shaping global norms and policies. This pluralization of governance actors can be positive, introducing new perspectives and expertise. However, it also raises questions about accountability, representation, and democratic legitimacy, especially when powerful corporate interests overshadow the voices of marginalized communities.

Garrad discusses the paradox at the heart of globalization: while it fosters interconnectedness and interdependence, it also generates backlash in the form of nationalism, protectionism, and populist movements that reject supranational institutions. This tension complicates efforts to build cohesive frameworks for global cooperation. The author concludes by suggesting that meaningful global governance will require reforming existing institutions to make them more representative, inclusive, and adaptable—while also empowering civil society and local communities to hold global actors accountable.

➔ Key Insights

- While globalization once meant Western-led trade and financial expansion, today's multipolar reality features multiple centers of economic power. This creates both opportunities for more diverse leadership and friction over fair representation.
- Nations remain protective of their autonomy — but issues like carbon emissions, digital privacy, and resource depletion require states to compromise and coordinate.
- The text calls for serious reforms in international institutions to reflect new power dynamics and build legitimacy among rising states and civil society.

Discussion Questions

1. In what ways did political motivations outweigh economic logic during the Cold War?
2. How has technological change contributed to both integration and inequality?
3. What are the major criticisms of institutions such as the IMF and WTO?
4. Should non-state actors have greater influence in global decision-making? Why or why not?
5. How can global governance be made more democratic and inclusive?
6. What historical events have most shaped the modern global economic order?

Key Terms and Concepts

Globalization – The increasing global interconnectedness through trade, investment, and technology.

Global Governance – Institutional processes for managing global affairs across borders.

Bretton Woods Institutions – IMF and World Bank, created post-WWII for economic stability.

Cold War – Geopolitical tension between U.S.-led and USSR-led blocs, shaping global economics.

Liberalization – Policy shift towards open markets and reduced government intervention.

Sovereignty – The right of a state to self-govern without external interference.

Non-State Actors – Influential entities in international affairs (e.g., NGOs, MNCs).

IMF (International Monetary Fund) – Offers financial aid and policy advice to countries.

WTO (World Trade Organization) – Regulates trade and resolves international disputes.

Inequality – Uneven access to resources, opportunities, and wealth across groups or nations.

Digital Divide – The gap in technology access between individuals and countries.

MNCs (Multinational Corporations) – Corporations operating in multiple countries.

Populism – Political movements claiming to represent the common people against elites.

NAFTA – A trilateral trade agreement between the U.S., Canada, and Mexico.

Institutional Legitimacy – The perceived fairness and accountability of governing institutions.

Learning Objectives

By the end of this chapter, students will be able to:

- Define the concept of civil society and explain how it has evolved into a global phenomenon.
- Describe the historical development of civil society from ancient times to modern global contexts.
- Analyze how globalization and digital technologies have expanded the reach of civil society.
- Evaluate the diverse paradigms that explain the nature and function of global civil society.
- Assess the impact of global crises like the COVID-19 pandemic on civil society's roles.
- Identify key challenges and opportunities for civil society in the 21st century.
- Reflect critically on the potential of global civil society to shape more democratic and inclusive global governance.

The Political Origins of Globalization and the Post-War World Order

In the modern era, the idea of civil society has come to represent a vital layer of organized social life that bridges the gap between individuals, the state, and the market. Civil society takes many forms: neighborhood associations, faith communities, labor unions, student groups, grassroots movements, professional networks, think tanks, and large international non-governmental organizations (NGOs). This vast diversity shows how civil society adapts to respond to both local and global challenges. As Scholte (2004) described, it is "a political space where voluntary associations seek, outside political parties, to shape the rules that govern one other aspect of social life" (p. 214).

What is remarkable today is that this sphere of voluntary action has expanded far beyond national borders into what is now widely referred to as global civil society. This term captures how activists, community leaders, and informal networks work across countries to tackle challenges that no single government can solve alone—whether defending human rights, responding to humanitarian disasters, fighting climate change, or demanding greater corporate responsibility. In this sense, global civil society both mirrors and shapes globalization itself, providing a counterbalance to the concentrated power of states and corporations.

The roots of civil society stretch deep into history. Ancient Roman thinkers like Cicero discussed the duties that citizens owe to the common good, setting early foundations for the idea that social life requires spaces of collective responsibility beyond rulers and markets. Later, early modern philosophers such as Thomas Hobbes and John Locke refined these ideas by arguing for a liberal vision in which individuals freely associate within a shared public sphere. During the Enlightenment, civil society was imagined as an arena separate from the state, where people could organize according to their own interests and values (Carothers & Barndt, 1999, p. 18). This vision flourished alongside the rise of capitalism and urbanization, as growing cities provided new spaces for people to gather and mobilize outside the reach of monarchs and expanding markets.

However, the concept of civil society did not evolve uniformly across cultures. In Asia, for instance, village councils and kinship-based mutual aid networks performed similar functions long before European liberalism formalized the notion of "civil society." In India, traditional panchayats and community-led social movements have historically provided mechanisms for conflict resolution and collective action that stand apart from state authority. In Africa, clan-based governance and religious brotherhoods have shaped local civic life, challenging the idea that civil society is purely a Western export.

During the Industrial Revolution, centralized governments and expanding markets overshadowed many smaller civic associations in the West. Yet the idea of civil society never fully disappeared. In the 20th century, it gained new life through the writings of the Italian theorist Antonio Gramsci, who argued that civil society is a cultural battleground—an arena for ideas, values, and beliefs, where dominant ideologies are reinforced but also contested. Gramsci's concept of "dictatorship plus hegemony" (Öncü, 2003) inspired later generations to see civil society not merely as a collection of charities or clubs but as a powerful space for resisting authoritarianism and promoting social change.

This became dramatically evident during the democratic transitions of the 1970s and 1980s, when civil society movements—labor unions, churches, student groups, and neighborhood organizations—played decisive roles in pushing back against dictatorship. In Eastern Europe, grassroots organizers gave civil society a heroic dimension as they helped bring down communist regimes. Carothers and Barndt noted that "Czech, Hungarian, and Polish activists also wrapped themselves in the banner of civil society, endowing it with a heroic quality when the Berlin Wall fell" (1999, p. 19). Similar stories played out in Latin America, where human rights groups and community organizations challenged oppressive military regimes and demanded democratic governance.

The same pattern has repeated in more recent struggles. In the Middle East and North Africa, the Arab Spring demonstrated both the potential and the perils of global civil society in the digital age. Civic groups and young activists used social media to mobilize mass protests and topple autocratic leaders. Yet the backlash was equally swift, with many movements crushed or co-opted by entrenched elites or military regimes. This shows that the expansion of civic space is never guaranteed; it must be defended continuously.

The Digital Turn and the Rise of Global Civil Society

In our time, the reach of civil society has expanded dramatically due to globalization and rapid technological change. As McGrew (1992) described, globalization means the "multiplicity of linkages and interconnections that transcend the nation-states." Advances in communication technology—satellite television, the internet, mobile devices, and social media—have made it far cheaper and faster for people to connect and coordinate across borders. Castells (2010) famously called this new reality the "network society," in which "the most dynamic social movements are connected via the Internet across the city, the country, and the world" (p. 248). Activists, researchers, and concerned citizens can now form coalitions that pressure governments and corporations on issues like landmines, forced labor, sweatshops, or carbon emissions.

One striking example of how civil society crosses borders is the global climate movement. Millions of young people have organized climate strikes inspired by Greta Thunberg's Fridays for Future, demanding accountability from corporations and governments alike. Similarly, movements like Extinction Rebellion have used nonviolent direct action to push climate policy higher on national and international agendas. These movements highlight the hybrid character of global civil society today: decentralized yet capable of capturing the world's attention through viral digital tactics and mass mobilization.

Yet this global reach is not evenly shared. While digital technologies have opened doors for many, they have left others behind. Millions of people still lack stable internet connections or the language and technical skills needed to engage in global conversations. Small community organizations often struggle to secure funding and visibility, while large international NGOs sometimes overshadow local voices or face accusations of promoting donor-driven agendas rather than genuine local priorities. The digital divide thus shapes who can participate fully in global civil society.

Scholars such as Mary Kaldor (2003) remind us that there is no single definition of global civil society because it wears many faces. Kaldor identifies three key ways of understanding it. First are the new social movements that emerged from the cultural shifts of 1968 onwards, championing issues such as gender equality, environmental justice, and peace through flexible, horizontal organizing structures. Second is the "new policy agenda," which describes how NGOs have increasingly become important partners for governments and international donors, delivering services and promoting democratic values—although this has sparked debates about whether civil society risks becoming an extension of foreign aid rather than an independent force for accountability and change. The third perspective is a postmodern view that emphasizes how global civil society is not exclusively Western or secular. Indigenous, faith-based, and identity-based networks play critical roles, sometimes resisting liberal norms or advancing alternative frameworks for justice and solidarity. As Kaldor argued, "Global civil society cannot be just the 'nice, good movements'" (2003, pp. 589–590).

Civil Society in Crisis and Transformation: Lessons from the COVID-19 Pandemic

The COVID-19 pandemic provided a vivid test of civil society's resilience and adaptability under unprecedented global stress. While many governments struggled to respond quickly or equitably, civil society organizations stepped in with remarkable speed and creativity. According to CIVICUS (2020), "CSOs worked not only as frontline responders, but also as defenders of human rights during the pandemic, including the rights of vulnerable and excluded groups" (p. 2). From neighborhood mutual aid networks delivering groceries to the elderly, to interfaith coalitions providing protective equipment and shelter, to global coalitions like Gavi and COVAX ensuring equitable vaccine distribution, civil society groups filled critical gaps left by overwhelmed or inactive states. Bhargava (2021) emphasized that local NGOs brought deep community knowledge that governments often lacked, helping reach marginalized communities quickly and fairly.

Yet the pandemic also revealed deep structural weaknesses within civil society. As lockdowns forced many activities online, grassroots groups with limited digital capacity were left scrambling. Organizations dependent on in-person fundraising or community gatherings saw their income streams vanish overnight. Meanwhile, some authoritarian regimes took advantage of the crisis to expand surveillance, limit freedom of assembly, and pass restrictive laws under the cover of public health emergency powers. Many groups that shifted rapidly to digital platforms found themselves exposed to cyber threats, harassment, and intrusive monitoring, highlighting a new frontier in the struggle for civic space: digital security.

Despite these pressures, the pandemic also spurred innovation. In many cities, volunteers organized mutual aid collectives to deliver food, medicine, and mental health support. Faith communities turned churches, mosques, and temples into pop-up clinics and information hubs. Youth networks used TikTok, Instagram, and messaging apps not only to share health information but to mobilize for vaccine equity, push back against misinformation, and advocate for marginalized groups often excluded from national pandemic responses. These creative forms of solidarity showed that civil society's strength does not only lie in large NGOs but also in the millions of micro-actions that connect neighbors, strangers, and distant communities through shared values and urgent needs.

Tensions and Strategies in a Globalized Civic Space

Looking forward, this adaptive capacity will be essential as civil society tackles the intertwined global crises of the 21st century. Climate change, rising inequality, migration, digital authoritarianism, and disinformation all demand responses that cross borders and silos. Local communities fighting deforestation or water pollution need allies in international advocacy networks. Women's rights activists challenging gender-based violence often find strength and legitimacy through global sisterhoods that share resources and amplify voices. Indigenous movements defending land and cultural rights increasingly use international forums, like UN bodies or transnational courts, to challenge national governments and extractive industries.

However, this global-local interplay is not without tension. Critics argue that large international NGOs can overshadow local actors, dominate funding streams, or promote donor-driven agendas that neglect grassroots realities. This has sparked ongoing debates within civil society about accountability, representation, and power imbalances. Some advocate for "localization"—a shift in resources, leadership, and decision-making to community-based organizations that hold deep cultural and contextual knowledge. Others point to the need for new partnership models that balance global influence with local legitimacy, avoiding a one-size-fits-all approach to transnational activism.

Security remains another central challenge. As digital surveillance grows more sophisticated, civic actors must invest in secure communication tools, digital literacy, and legal frameworks that protect data privacy and freedom of expression. The role of "infosec" (information security) professionals and civic technologists has become vital. Coalitions like the Electronic Frontier Foundation and Access Now have emerged as defenders of digital rights, pushing for policy reforms and supporting activists with training and secure platforms. As the line between online and offline activism blurs, civil society's ability to protect itself in the digital realm will determine whether it can continue to serve as a check on power in the physical world.

Legitimacy, too, must be renewed continuously. Large NGOs are under pressure to demonstrate that they truly represent the communities they claim to serve, rather than acting as elite gatekeepers to donor funds and international platforms. Participatory governance, community-led monitoring, and bottom-up leadership development are becoming essential strategies to build and maintain trust. In this sense, civil society's legitimacy is not given once and for all; it is relational, fragile, and earned through actions that resonate with the people whose lives they seek to improve.

Encouragingly, there are signs that civil society is adapting to these demands. Networks like CIVICUS and regional alliances such as the African Platform on Civic Space are experimenting with new models for accountability and collective voice. Feminist movements, LGBTQ+ coalitions, disability rights groups, and Indigenous communities are challenging mainstream NGOs to move beyond token inclusion toward real power-sharing and co-leadership. This internal pluralism—sometimes messy and conflictual—can be a source of renewal, pushing civil society to live up to its democratic ideals.

Rethinking Power, Partnerships, and the Future of Global Civil Society

Another frontier for global civil society is its relationship with the private sector. As public trust in governments and corporations shifts, many NGOs have forged partnerships with ethical businesses, social enterprises, and technology companies. These partnerships bring opportunities for funding, innovation, and wider reach but also pose risks of co-optation and mission drift. Striking the right balance—collaborating without losing independence—remains an ongoing tension. The rise of corporate social responsibility (CSR), impact investing, and social impact metrics reflects how civil society's advocacy has shaped business norms, but it also requires vigilance to ensure that profit-driven interests do not dilute deeper commitments to justice and sustainability.

Amid these trends, young people are reshaping what global civil society looks like. From school strikes for climate to digital feminist campaigns like #MeToo, youth-led networks have shown that they can mobilize millions, reframe narratives, and force political leaders to listen. Unlike older hierarchical NGOs, many of these movements operate through loose, decentralized structures that resist formalization. This can make them harder to co-opt but also raises questions about sustainability, resource distribution, and long-term strategy. Nonetheless, they inject fresh energy and moral urgency into global civil society, reminding the world that radical imagination and collective action remain powerful tools for change.

In the end, global civil society is neither static nor uniform. It is an ever-evolving, pluralistic ecosystem of people and groups who believe that democracy, rights, and justice cannot be left solely to markets or states. Its enduring strength lies in its adaptability—its capacity to learn, self-criticize, renew alliances, and imagine alternatives when old systems fail. As Brechenmacher et al. (2020) concluded, civil society remains "a critical counteractive to government and market let-downs; a steadfast partner, and a dynamic source of care, leadership, and accountability" (p. 15).

For this ecosystem to thrive in the 21st century, it must hold itself to the same standards it demands of others: transparency, inclusion, accountability, and solidarity across borders and identities. It must cultivate resilience against digital and political threats while embracing the creative potential of new generations and new tools. It must protect civic space not as a privilege for a few but as a universal right for all. If it succeeds, global civil society will continue to be not just a mirror of globalization but a force that shapes it toward a more just, democratic, and humane future.

Related Article to Read:

Erasmus, C.-L., & Glencorse, B. (2025, February 24). Why businesses must step up to sustain global civil society. World Economic Forum. https://www.weforum.org/stories/2025/02/why-businesses-sustain-global-civil-society/

➔ Key Summary

In their article "Why Businesses Must Step Up to Sustain Global Civil Society" (World Economic Forum, 2025), Erasmus and Glencorse argue that the survival of vibrant global civil society is increasingly dependent on proactive engagement and support from the private sector. The piece highlights that in an era marked by shrinking civic space, rising authoritarianism, funding cuts for NGOs, and erosion of public trust, businesses have both an ethical stake and a practical interest in sustaining the civic environments that underpin democracy, rule of law, and stable markets.

The authors contend that civil society provides public goods that governments and markets alone cannot deliver—such as independent oversight, human rights protection, environmental advocacy, and community resilience. These civic functions are foundational to creating societies where businesses can operate predictably and communities can thrive. Yet many NGOs and community-based organizations now face funding shortfalls, legal restrictions, and security threats that jeopardize their ability to function independently.

The article calls on companies to view support for civil society not as a charitable add-on but as a core strategic investment. The authors emphasize that companies benefit when civil society is strong: watchdogs that hold governments accountable also ensure that the playing field remains fair and corruption is checked, which supports long-term business continuity and good governance. Furthermore, a robust civil society builds trust and legitimacy in contexts where businesses seek to expand operations, manage supply chains, or address social and environmental challenges.

Examples in the article show how some corporations are already stepping up through partnerships, grant-making, advocacy for civic freedoms, and by using their influence to resist anti-democratic trends. The authors point to innovative cross-sector collaborations where companies, foundations, and civil society organizations co-design solutions to complex challenges like climate change, labor rights, and social inclusion. They stress, however, that such partnerships must be trust-based, transparent, and grounded in mutual respect—avoiding the risk of co-optation or "CSR-washing."

Erasmus and Glencorse also warn that businesses must go beyond surface-level commitments. Real impact requires integrating support for civic space into core business practices—embedding human rights due diligence, protecting whistleblowers, ensuring ethical supply chains, and publicly defending civic freedoms when they come under attack.

The piece concludes that as governments retreat from funding or even actively suppress civil society, the private sector has a unique opportunity and responsibility to help fill this gap. By backing civil society, businesses protect the social license that makes open markets possible and demonstrate leadership in defending the inclusive, just, and resilient societies on which long-term economic growth depends.

➔ Key Insights

- When governments reduce or freeze international aid, communities lose vital support for civic actors, journalists, and local NGOs.
- Closing civic space undermines democratic institutions, which in turn destabilizes business operations and market predictability.
- Forward-looking businesses increasingly recognize that strengthening civil society is not philanthropy alone—it is a strategic investment in their operating environment.

- Corporate social responsibility should go beyond compliance and charity; it should include defending civic freedoms and supporting local organizations through funding and partnership.

Discussion Questions

1. How has the concept of civil society evolved from ancient and Enlightenment ideas to today's global civil society?
2. In what ways has globalization transformed the scale and influence of civil society actors?
3. How do digital technologies both empower and endanger civil society organizations?
4. Compare Kaldor's three paradigms of global civil society. Which paradigm do you think is most visible today?
5. How did civil society organizations respond differently from governments during the COVID-19 pandemic?
6. What are the main challenges for civil society to maintain legitimacy and accountability while operating globally?
7. How can global civil society help strengthen democracy and human rights in the future?

Key Terms and Concepts

Civil Society – Voluntary associations that operate independently of the state to promote common interests.

Global Civil Society – A network of civic actors working across borders on transnational issues.

Network Society – A term coined by Castells to describe society structured by digital and communication networks.

New Social Movements (NSMs) – Grassroots movements focused on post-materialist values like ecology, gender, and peace.

New Policy Agenda (NPA) – The idea that NGOs support governance by filling state capacity gaps.

Postmodern Paradigm – A view that recognizes diverse and non-Western forms of civil society.

NGOs – Non-governmental organizations that work in advocacy, service delivery, or development.

Transnational Advocacy Networks – Civil society coalitions that operate across countries.

CIVICUS – A global alliance that monitors civic space and supports civil society engagement.

Bhargava (2021) – A scholar who emphasized CSO participation in COVID-19 vaccine governance.

Gavi & COVAX – Global platforms involving CSOs in vaccine distribution.

Digital Divide – The gap in access to digital tools between rich and poor populations.

Mutual Aid – Community-based networks for reciprocal support.

Accountability – The obligation of CSOs to be transparent and responsive to stakeholders.

Gramsci – Italian theorist who analyzed civil society as a site of ideological struggle.

Reference

Bhargava, V. (2021). *Engaging Civil Society Organizations to Enhance the Effectiveness of COVID-19 Response Programs in Asia and the Pacific* (Governance Brief No. 42). Asian Development Bank.

Brechenmacher, S., Carothers, T., & Youngs, R. (2020). *Civil Society and the Coronavirus: Dynamism Despite Disruption*. Carnegie Endowment for International Peace.

Carothers, T., & Barndt, W. (1999). Civil society. *Foreign Policy*, (117), 18–29.

Castells, M. (2010). Towards a sociology of the network society. In G. Ritzer & Z. Atalay (Eds.), *Readings in globalization: Key concepts and major debates* (pp. 246–252). Wiley-Blackwell.

CIVICUS. (2020). *Solidarity in the time of COVID-19: Civil society responses to the pandemic.*

Gonzalez-Perez, M. A. (2013). Global civil society and international business: A review. In M. A. Gonzalez-Perez & L. Leonard (Eds.), *International business, sustainability and corporate social responsibility* (Vol. 11, pp. 37–63). Emerald Group Publishing.

Kaldor, M. (2003). The idea of global civil society. *International Affairs*, 79(3), 583–593.

Leyshon, A. (1995). Annihilating space?: The speed-up of communications. In J. Allen & C. Hamnett (Eds.), *A shrinking world?: Global unevenness and inequality* (pp. 11–54). Oxford University Press.

McGrew, T. (1992). A global society? In S. Hall, D. Held, & T. McGrew (Eds.), *Modernity and its futures* (pp. 61–116). Polity Press.

Öncü, A. (2003). Dictatorship plus hegemony: A Gramscian analysis of the Turkish state. *Science & Society*, 67(3), 303–328.

Scholte, J. A. (2004). Civil society and democratically accountable global governance. *Government and Opposition*, 39(2), 211–233.

Learning Objectives

By the end of this chapter, students will be able to:

- Explain the concept of global citizenship and its historical evolution.
- Identify the core values and principles that underpin global citizenship education (GCED).
- Analyze the role of transnational NGOs in advancing global citizenship.
- Evaluate the importance of youth engagement in shaping a peaceful, inclusive, and sustainable world.
- Reflect critically on how global citizenship can address global challenges such as extremism, inequality, and climate change.

A World of Interconnected Challenges and the Case for Global Citizenship

In today's deeply interdependent world, we face challenges that no single country can address alone. Conflicts persist across many regions, forcing millions of people to flee their homes and creating ripple effects that threaten peace and security far beyond any national border. Alongside these conflicts, rising violent extremism, entrenched poverty, stark gender and economic inequalities, the worsening climate crisis, and the plight of refugees and internally displaced persons all serve as stark reminders of how interconnected our problems have become. These complex issues demand more than just policy coordination; they require a deep shift in the mindsets, attitudes, and shared values that shape how people relate to each other across cultures, nations, and continents.

As United Nations Secretary-General António Guterres has stressed, peace and conflict prevention remain "one of the most important and urgent agenda items for the United Nations." Recognizing this, the concept of "sustaining peace," first emphasized in landmark UN resolutions in 2016, urges us to go beyond reactive crisis management. Instead, it calls for addressing root causes of conflict and investing in post-conflict reconstruction and reconciliation. This approach is built on the understanding that true, lasting peace is not secured by diplomacy and military interventions alone—it depends on transforming how individuals and communities see themselves in relation to one another and the wider world.

Against this backdrop, the idea of global citizenship has gained renewed traction as an important framework for tackling these challenges. According to UNESCO, global citizenship education (GCED) "aims to empower learners to engage and assume active roles, both locally and globally, to face and resolve global challenges and ultimately to become proactive contributors to a more just, peaceful, tolerant, inclusive, secure and sustainable world" (UNESCO, 2015). This vision invites people to expand their sense of civic responsibility beyond the borders of the nation-state and embrace a broader identity that ties them to a global community.

The Principles and Practice of Global Citizenship Education (GCED)

As Schattle (2007) famously noted, "National citizenship is an accident of birth; global citizenship is different. It is a voluntary association with a concept that signifies ways of thinking and living within multiple cross-cutting communities—cities, regions, states, nations, and international collectives." This means that global citizenship is not something one inherits by birthright. It is a conscious commitment, nurtured by education, intercultural exposure, dialogue, and active participation in public life. Global citizenship demands that we see ourselves as part of a shared humanity, develop an understanding of the complex interdependence that binds us, and acquire the knowledge, skills, and values needed to contribute to peaceful and sustainable communities.

UNESCO's framework outlines three dimensions that are central to global citizenship: recognizing human dignity and universal values; cultivating respectful, healthy relationships across cultures, religions, and backgrounds; and embracing responsibility for sustainability and stewardship of the planet. These dimensions echo the core principles laid out in the influential Delors Report (1996), which described education for the twenty-first century as built on four pillars: "learning to know, learning to do, learning to be, and learning to live together."

Mutual respect and understanding are fundamental to healthy relationships. They start with developing cultural empathy and the skills to navigate diversity with openness and curiosity. This is particularly vital today, when hate speech, xenophobia, and extremist ideologies can spread globally in an instant via social media. As one international educator observed, "it is difficult to teach intercultural understanding to students who are unaware they, too, live in a culture that colors their perceptions." Thus, self-awareness is just as critical as awareness of others. It provides a foundation for countering prejudice, disinformation, and polarization.

Moreover, relationships with those who are marginalized or vulnerable demand not just empathy but solidarity and action. Learners are challenged to understand the commitment embedded in the Sustainable Development Goals (SDGs) to "leave no one behind." This means moving beyond seeing inequality as an abstract statistic to recognizing its human impact and working actively to promote social justice and human rights in their own communities and beyond.

Equally crucial is the relationship between people and the planet. Climate change and environmental degradation starkly demonstrate that our well-being is bound to the health of ecosystems that transcend national borders. Environmental stewardship is therefore not only an ecological necessity but a moral responsibility. Global citizenship education encourages learners to see themselves as caretakers of Earth's resources, to make informed, responsible choices, and to advocate for sustainability both locally and globally.

NGOs and Youth as Catalysts of Global Citizenship

Transnational NGOs have long played a critical role in advancing these principles of global citizenship. Unlike states, which are constrained by national interests and political calculations, NGOs can often act more flexibly, working directly with local communities, mobilizing resources quickly, and bringing marginalized voices to international platforms. For example, Amnesty International defends human rights worldwide, Greenpeace campaigns relentlessly for climate action, and Médecins Sans

Frontières provides essential medical care in conflict zones and disaster areas where state services often fail.

These organizations do far more than deliver aid. They are also crucial educators and mobilizers. Many NGOs partner with schools and universities to develop curricula that integrate global themes, train educators in GCED principles, and offer students practical experiences through volunteering, internships, and community service. They create real-life spaces where young people can explore how local action connects to global outcomes, learn by doing, and discover their power as engaged citizens.

Young people today are at the forefront of this movement. Across the globe, youth-led initiatives are demanding stronger action on climate change, gender equality, racial justice, and human rights. From Greta Thunberg's Fridays for Future to student campaigns for fair trade and sustainable cities, young people are using digital tools and creative tactics to hold governments and corporations accountable. This activism embodies the core spirit of global citizenship: a belief that young people are not passive observers but active agents of change, capable of shaping their communities and the world.

Risks, Resilience, and the Role of Education

However, this potential is not without threats. Many young people experience alienation and a sense of powerlessness in societies marked by rising inequality and political polarization. Extremist groups exploit this vulnerability, recruiting young people through sophisticated online campaigns that offer a sense of belonging. For example, the Islamic State in Iraq and the Levant (ISIL) attracted an estimated 40,000 foreign fighters from over 100 countries, many recruited via digital platforms. As the UN has noted, "The worldview and mindset of young people, as well as their sense of identity and belonging, are often weak and low. Now the orientation of education matters, and not just its quality."

Countering these threats demands that education foster resilience and critical thinking. Learners need strong digital literacy skills to recognize misinformation, resist propaganda, and use technology responsibly. They also need opportunities for genuine dialogue—safe spaces where they can debate ideas, question assumptions, and build trust across divides of culture, belief, and identity.

This is why innovative teaching methods are so important. UNESCO and partner organizations advocate for interactive, participatory learning approaches that go far beyond rote memorization. Techniques like structured debates, peer-to-peer projects, collaborative art and music, intercultural exchanges, and service learning help students practice empathy, communication, cooperation, and creative problem-solving. Field trips, community engagement, and international study experiences anchor theory in lived reality, showing learners that they are not powerless bystanders but co-creators of a shared future.

Building a Shared Future: Ethical Dialogue and Collective Responsibility

At an institutional level, collaboration is key. Governments can play a decisive role by designing supportive policies and allocating resources that embed global citizenship education into national education strategies. Schools and universities can integrate global themes across curricula—not as optional electives but as core components of what it means to be an educated person in the 21st century. NGOs can bridge the gap between the classroom and the wider community, offering practical pathways for students to live out the values of global citizenship in real life.

Yet persistent questions remain. Who decides which values are "universal"? How can educators respect cultural differences while promoting shared principles like human rights and sustainability? What happens when global citizenship appears to conflict with national identity or local traditions? These are not trivial concerns; they require honest, inclusive dialogue. They remind us that global citizenship must be an ongoing conversation, constantly shaped by diverse perspectives rather than dictated by any single dominant worldview.

As Altinay (2010) put it, "Navigating the treacherous waters of our epic interdependence requires a set of guiding principles that will shape ethical and fair responses." Education remains the best place for these principles to be taught, tested, and lived in practice.

The stakes could hardly be higher. "The future of humanity and of our planet lies in our hands. It lies also in the hands of today's younger generation who will pass the torch to future generations" (United Nations, 2015, para. 53). If we fail to prepare young people with the knowledge, skills, and values of global citizenship, we risk leaving them unprepared for the immense challenges they will inherit.

But if we succeed—if we build schools, communities, and civic spaces that nurture empathy, solidarity, resilience, and critical thinking—then global citizenship will be more than a distant ideal. It will become the foundation for a world that is more peaceful, inclusive, just, and sustainable. It will bring to life the aspirations enshrined in the SDGs, the UNESCO Constitution, and countless international declarations, transforming them from words on paper into real, everyday actions.

In this sense, global citizenship is not simply a moral aspiration—it is a practical necessity. It calls on each of us to look beyond ourselves and our borders, to affirm the dignity of every human being, and to work together to protect the only home we share.

Related Article to Read:

United Nations Chronicle. (n.d.). The Role of Civil Society in Advancing Global Citizenship. Retrieved from https://www.un.org/en/chronicle/article/role-civil-society-advancing-global-citizenship

➔ Key Summary

This UN Chronicle article explores how civil society organizations (CSOs)—from grassroots community groups to large transnational NGOs—are playing an increasingly indispensable role in promoting global citizenship. The piece argues that, while governments and multilateral institutions set the formal frameworks for cooperation and education, civil society often acts as the innovative frontline for testing what global citizenship can look like in practice.

Through local projects, global campaigns, intercultural dialogues, and non-formal education, CSOs create spaces where people learn to see themselves not only as members of a nation-state but also as part of a shared global community. These groups build solidarity across cultures, foster empathy, and advocate for human rights and environmental stewardship as fundamental aspects of being a responsible global citizen.

The article highlights how civil society's work often fills gaps left by the state or market, especially when it comes to addressing inequality, discrimination, and marginalization. By organizing communities, amplifying marginalized voices, and pushing for inclusive policies, civil society strengthens the social fabric necessary for meaningful global citizenship. It also emphasizes that civil society must remain flexible and experimental, adapting to local contexts while building bridges to global action.

Importantly, the piece stresses that global citizenship is not a static identity but an ongoing practice—a way of understanding, caring, and acting on behalf of people and the planet, often against a backdrop of increasing nationalism, xenophobia, and retreat from multilateralism. In this sense, the responsibility of civil society is to nurture civic imagination, create new narratives of solidarity, and hold governments and corporations accountable to the ideals of a just, sustainable, and peaceful world.

➔ Key Insights

- Civil society as pioneer: It often invents and tests grassroots paths to global awareness before formal institutions catch up.
- Education and dialogue: NGOs and CBOs are central to intercultural education—building empathy and capacity for global challenges.
- Networks matter: Through transnational partnerships, civil society amplifies local initiatives into global movements.

Discussion Questions

1. Why is global citizenship critical in today's global context?
2. How can GCED address root causes of radicalization and violence?
3. How do transnational NGOs promote global citizenship differently from national governments?
4. What roles can youth play in advancing global citizenship?
5. How does the "leave no one behind" principle connect to the ethics of global citizenship?

Key Terms and Concepts

Global Citizenship – A sense of belonging to a broader community and common humanity beyond national borders, encompassing responsibility toward global issues.

Global Citizenship Education (GCED) – Educational framework that empowers learners to engage with global challenges and promote justice, peace, and sustainability.

Delors Report – UNESCO report (1996) that defines four pillars of education: learning to know, to do, to be, and to live together.

Transnational NGOs – Non-governmental organizations that operate across borders to address global issues like human rights, education, and environmental protection.

UNESCO – United Nations Educational, Scientific and Cultural Organization, leading GCED efforts globally.

Youth Engagement – Involvement of young people as agents of social change, particularly through education and civic participation.

SDG 4.7 – Sustainable Development Goal target that promotes education for sustainable development and global citizenship.

Human Dignity – Core value in global citizenship, emphasizing respect for the worth of all individuals.

Sustainable Development – A development model that meets current needs without compromising future generations' ability to meet their own.

Reference

Altinay, H. (2010). Global civics: *Responsibilities and rights in an interconnected world.* Brookings Institution Press.

Delors, J., et al. (1996). *Learning: The treasure within.* Report to UNESCO of the International Commission on Education for the Twenty-first Century. UNESCO Publishing.

Green, M. F. (2012). Global citizenship: What are we talking about and why does it matter? *Trends and Insights for International Education Leaders.* NAFSA.

Nussbaum, M. C. (1997). *Cultivating humanity: A classical defense of reform in liberal education.* Harvard University Press.

Olson, C. L., Evans, R., & Shoenberg, R. (2007). *At home in the world: Bridging the gap between internationalization and multicultural education.* American Council on Education.

Schattle, H. (2007). *The practices of global citizenship.* Rowman & Littlefield.

UNESCO. (2015). *Global Citizenship Education: Topics and Learning Objectives.* Paris: UNESCO.

United Nations. (2015). *Transforming our world: The 2030 Agenda for Sustainable Development.* New York: United Nations.

Learning Objectives

By the end of this chapter, students will be able to:

- Describe the historical roots of international NGOs and explain their evolution from the abolitionist era to the present.
- Analyze how technological and geopolitical shifts have influenced the scale and strategies of NGO activities.
- Discuss the relationship between NGOs, states, and multinational enterprises in providing collective goods and shaping global governance.
- Evaluate the opportunities and challenges that arise from NGO branding, professionalization, and internationalization.
- Critically assess the role of NGOs as democratic actors, watchdogs, and partners in today's interconnected global society.

Historical Foundations of NGOs and Their Early Global Role

The idea that non-governmental organizations (NGOs) have become more influential only recently is misleading if we ignore their deep historical roots. From the abolitionist campaigns of the nineteenth century to the environmental, human rights, and humanitarian movements of today, NGOs have long shaped transnational ideas and inspired legal and moral shifts far beyond their modest institutional beginnings.

The nineteenth century abolitionist movement stands out as an early example of a global civil movement rooted in moral outrage and organized voluntary action. "Peace, labor, and free trade were major issues," and religious charities worked across colonies to deliver "charity, education, health, women, and children" services (Lan, 2018). These early campaigns laid the groundwork for what we now recognize as the global civil society space—a realm that Scholte (2004) famously described as "a political space where voluntary associations seek, outside political parties, to shape the rules that govern one other aspect of social life."

The power of NGOs to influence formal international law emerged strikingly through individuals like Henri Dunant, who turned the horrors he witnessed into a catalyst for change. As documented, "A man, shocked by an event he witnessed, decided that change was an urgent moral imperative... He wrote a book that triggered the creation of an international NGO," the International Committee of the Red Cross, which lobbied successfully for the first Geneva Convention of 1864—an act that launched the field of modern international humanitarian law.

Expansion in the 20th Century: From War Relief to Global Movements

The twentieth century brought new drivers of NGO formation and expansion. In the ashes of two world wars, humanitarian aid organizations flourished to respond to mass displacement, poverty, and the moral imperative of rebuilding war-torn societies. The Cold War era then catalyzed another wave of activism: "movements for human rights, feminism, peace, and environmental protection began to emerge and various social forces asserted their influence" (Lan, 2018). This surge reflected the pressures and contradictions of post-industrial societies grappling with nuclear tensions and new global interdependencies.

By the 1980s and 1990s, NGOs entered a phase of "exponential growth" (Lan, 2018). This expansion was not accidental—it was fueled by European Union investments and a reconfiguration of global development finance. As Siméant (2005) notes, the creation of the European Commission's Humanitarian Office (ECHO) helped formalize the role of European NGOs as key actors in global relief and development. This shift institutionalized NGOs as official partners in global governance frameworks—channeling public and private resources into organized civil action on a scale unseen in previous centuries.

Technology, Visibility, and the Rise of Global Civil Action

At the same time, new technologies democratized access to transnational organizing. While many assume the Internet was purely a military invention, its opening to civil society owed much to NGO pioneers who foresaw its potential. "Contrary to popular belief," the Internet's role in NGO work did not start with governments but with "a small number of NGO activists in the 1980s who realized the potential of electronic communications to enhance the work of all NGOs." (Original source) By the mid-

1980s, networks like Interdoc and APC laid the groundwork for civil society's digital transformation, paving the way for real-time global collaboration decades before hashtags and viral campaigns defined online activism.

This technological leap meant that "global communications can for the first time be used by the poor as well as the rich," evidenced dramatically by the peasants of Narmada, India, who mounted an international Internet-based campaign to stop World Bank funding for a dam that threatened to flood their ancestral lands. (Original text) Such stories underline that for many marginalized communities, digital platforms became lifelines for transnational solidarity.

As NGOs grew in size and reach, they adapted their identity to the era of branding and visibility. Laidler-Kylander et al. (2007) emphasize that "An NGO brand needs to display the present mission of the organization, because it embodies the reason behind the NGOs' existence." But crafting and defending a coherent global brand is complex. Decentralized structures, cultural diversity, and informal hierarchies can make it hard to project a unified identity, particularly when scandals or controversial partnerships threaten to erode trust built painstakingly over decades.

Behind these brands are diverse stakeholders—individual donors, institutional funders, volunteers, local communities—each with their own expectations. As NGOs professionalize, they increasingly rely on skilled managers and specialized staff to run projects across continents. This professionalization trend means that while volunteerism remains vital, many large NGOs today look and operate more like sophisticated development agencies than grassroots charities.

Yet as NGOs professionalize, they face the risk of becoming distant from the very communities they seek to serve. Lan (2018) notes that "As NGOs grow, they are more project-oriented… spending much of their time and resources on managing these projects," which often shifts their center of gravity away from local grassroots engagement toward donor-driven priorities and compliance requirements.

Complex Partnerships: States, Markets, and Questions of Legitimacy

The tightrope NGOs walk between independence and partnership is nowhere more evident than in their relationship with states. As Bouget and Prouteau (2002) describe, NGO-state relations range from strict control to relative autonomy. In the Cold War and post-Cold War period, NGOs shifted from "direct charitable aid" to more strategic roles, including policy advocacy and public service delivery. This created both opportunities and dilemmas: governments see NGOs as efficient and flexible, especially where state capacity is weak, but NGOs risk being co-opted if they rely too heavily on state funding.

This blurred line between public and private spheres has pushed NGOs to develop new forms of legitimacy. For example, Boddewyn and Doh (2011) argue that NGOs often act as bridges to fill "institutional voids"—providing collective goods such as health, education, and clean water in contexts where states and markets fail to deliver. In emerging economies, these collaborations are vital but fraught with tensions over accountability, power imbalances, and the risk of NGOs becoming service providers without the capacity to challenge structural injustices.

The interplay between NGOs and multinational enterprises (MNEs) adds another layer of complexity. Corporations partner with NGOs to secure local legitimacy, manage risk, or co-deliver projects in fragile contexts. NGOs, in turn, gain resources and leverage to expand their reach. But these partnerships also test NGOs' independence, raising ethical questions about how watchdogs can also be collaborators.

Amid this institutional complexity, the idea of NGOs as democratic agents sparks ongoing debate. Many activists claim NGOs can serve as "the voice of the people," but critics note that "many highly respected NGOs do not have any mechanisms for internal democracy." (Original text) Unlike elected governments, they do not speak for majorities but rather for self-selecting, often highly motivated constituencies.

Despite these limits, NGOs undeniably strengthen global democracy by making power visible and contestable. As the original text notes, "NGOs immensely enhance the flow of information in global governance." They bring neglected issues to diplomatic tables, challenge governments to live up to international promises, and foster public debate that might otherwise remain hidden behind closed doors.

This dual role—insider and outsider, watchdog and partner—is vividly illustrated in human rights battles. The struggle to include human rights language in the UN Charter in 1945, the 1970 breakthrough "1503 procedure," and Amnesty International's long fight that led to the Convention against Torture in 1984 all show how sustained civil society pressure can reshape norms and bend the arc of international law.

The Road Ahead: Global Reach, Accountability, and Moral Leadership

Today, NGOs also face mounting demands to adapt how they operate. They must find new ways to "encourage the sharing of the best practices and knowledge between countries; support the process of commonly planning a global brand; allocate responsibilities to create synergies; and perform brand-building strategies to the best of their abilities" (Laidler-Kylander et al., 2007). They must navigate the rise of social enterprise models, leverage new technologies, and respond to calls for transparency from stakeholders who expect professional accountability alongside moral clarity.

Finally, NGOs are pushed by globalization itself. Many started as local efforts, but crises, donor incentives, and the logic of global interdependence propelled them outward. Lee and Han (2020) point out that "the international expansion of NGOs is mainly due to the demand to provide their services on wider geographic horizons and to find new donors in order to increase their competitiveness." Social movements, foreign partnerships, and cross-border advocacy campaigns all show that the internationalization of NGOs is as much about networks and trust as it is about formal strategy.

In a world of eroding trust in traditional institutions, NGOs remind us that the power of organized people can still challenge the status quo. Their survival depends on managing old tensions—independence versus partnership, local roots versus global reach, moral clarity versus political compromise. The questions remain: How can NGOs maintain credibility and boldness in the face of co-optation? How can they defend their values while navigating complex alliances with states and markets? And how can they sustain the fierce, disruptive energy that made them powerful in the first place?

If history is a guide, the answer lies in their ability to adapt, connect, and inspire. NGOs continue to show that the pursuit of justice, dignity, and solidarity can transcend borders, outlast empires, and reshape the moral horizon of what is possible.

Related Article to Read:

Davies, T. R. (2020). NGOs and transnational non-state politics. E-International Relations. Retrieved from https://www.e-ir.info/2020/10/02/ngos-and-transnational-non-state-politics/

Key Summary

In "NGOs and Transnational Non-State Politics", Thomas Davies explains how NGOs have become central actors in global politics by operating far beyond traditional state boundaries and institutions. He shows that NGOs no longer simply lobby governments or participate as observers in intergovernmental forums, they now directly shape international norms, set standards, provide essential services, and build cross-border networks that rival the influence of states. NGOs target corporations and private actors, using tactics like global consumer campaigns or shareholder activism to push for changes in supply chains, labor conditions, or environmental standards—sometimes achieving results faster than formal state negotiations could. They have also built systems of private governance through certifications such as FairTrade or the Forest Stewardship Council, which create de facto global rules for ethical production and sustainability. These transnational standards often fill regulatory gaps left by weak or fragmented state action.

Davies highlights how NGOs frequently step in to provide critical services like healthcare, education, or humanitarian aid, especially in regions where states are absent, fragile, or unwilling to act. Organizations such as Médecins Sans Frontières and the International Planned Parenthood Federation deliver direct services that millions depend on, blurring the line between civil society and governance. Beyond service delivery, NGOs build entire parallel spaces for civic engagement through networks and movements that link activists, scholars, and communities across borders—such as the World Social Forum or global feminist and climate justice coalitions. These networks strengthen civil society's capacity to resist domination by powerful states or corporations and offer alternative visions of how global challenges can be addressed.

Yet Davies also notes that this expansion creates tensions. Large, well-funded international NGOs often have more resources and visibility than local grassroots groups, raising concerns about whose voices are amplified and who sets priorities. Reliance on donor funding or corporate partnerships can create risks that NGOs lose independence or align too closely with business interests. Nonetheless, the COVID-19 pandemic illustrated how indispensable transnational non-state actors have become. When governments failed to respond quickly, NGOs mobilized resources, shared critical information, and coordinated emergency relief across borders.

Ultimately, Davies argues that to understand contemporary global governance, we must look beyond states and formal institutions and pay closer attention to how NGOs and other non-state networks shape what counts as acceptable behavior, who gets heard, and how global norms evolve in practice. NGOs are no longer just supporting actors; they have become architects of transnational rules, providers of essential goods, and powerful connectors of people, ideas, and movements that challenge the limits of state-centric governance.

➲ Key Insights

- Expanded political reach: NGOs now target non-state actors—businesses, individuals—shifting beyond traditional diplomatic influence.
- Institution-building capacity: Through standard-setting and certification schemes, NGOs co-govern global systems.
- Crisis resilience: COVID-19 revealed both the fragility of conventional state systems and NGOs' adaptive role in service provision and advocacy.
- Counterbalance to inequality: NGOs can create alternative "parallel societies" that challenge formal power, though this may also introduce sustainability and equity issues.

Discussion Questions

1. How did early campaigns like the abolitionist movement and the creation of the Red Cross shape the foundation of modern NGOs?
2. In what ways did technology and digital networks transform the reach and influence of NGOs?
3. Why do some scholars argue that NGOs cannot fully represent 'the voice of the people'? Do you agree?
4. How does the relationship between NGOs and states both strengthen and threaten NGO independence?
5. What are the risks and rewards of NGOs embracing global branding and professionalized structures?
6. How can NGOs balance local grassroots accountability with global scale and partnerships with corporations or governments?
7. Reflecting on examples like Amnesty International's anti-torture campaign, what does this reveal about the power of sustained civil pressure in shaping international law?

Key Terms and Concepts

Abolitionist Movement – A historic campaign to end slavery, often seen as a precursor to modern human rights NGOs.

International Committee of the Red Cross (ICRC) – One of the first major humanitarian NGOs, instrumental in creating the Geneva Conventions.

Geneva Convention – Landmark treaties establishing standards for humanitarian treatment during war.

Global Civil Society – A transnational sphere of voluntary associations shaping global norms beyond the nation-state.

Interdoc & APC (Association for Progressive Communications) – Early NGO networks that expanded digital activism and global electronic communications.

NGO Branding – The strategic use of brand identity to maintain public trust and donor support.

Professionalization – The shift from volunteer-led models to employing paid staff, managers, and experts.

Institutional Voids – Situations where states fail to provide public goods, creating space for NGOs and businesses to step in.

Collective Goods – Essential goods/services like health, education, water, or energy provided to communities.

Social Capital – The value generated by building networks of trust and collaboration.

Liabilities of Newness, Smallness, and Foreignness – Challenges NGOs face when expanding internationally, such as lack of resources or local legitimacy.

Reference

Boddewyn, J., & Doh, J. (2011). Global strategy and the collaboration of MNEs, NGOs, and governments for the provisioning of collective goods in emerging markets. *Global Strategy Journal*, 1, 345–361.

Bouget, D., & Prouteau, L. (2002). National and supranational government-NGO relations: Anti-discrimination policy formation in the European Union. *Public Administration and Development*, 22(1), 31–37.

Galkina, T., & Yang, M. (2020). Bringing Nordic slush to Asia: Entrepreneurial internationalization of an NGO as a social movement. *International Business Review*, 29(4), 101749.

Laidler-Kylander, N., Quelch, J. A., & Simonin, B. L. (2007). Building and valuing global brands in the nonprofit sector. *Nonprofit Management and Leadership*, 17(3), 253–277.

Lan, Y. (2018). History and paradigm shift: NGOs in international development aid. *China Nonprofit Review*, 10(1), 108–133.

Siméant, J. (2005). What is going global? The internationalization of French NGOs 'without borders'. *Review of International Political Economy*, 12(5), 851–883.

Teegen, H. (2003). International NGOs as global institutions: Using social capital to impact multinational enterprises and governments. *Journal of International Management*, 9(3), 271–285.

Learning Objectives

By the end of this chapter, students will be able to:

- Explain the historical and contemporary role of NGOs in shaping global governance.
- Analyze how NGOs have used technology to expand their influence and overcome barriers.
- Evaluate the relationship between NGOs and intergovernmental institutions such as the United Nations.
- Discuss the challenges NGOs face regarding legitimacy, representation, and democratic accountability.
- Reflect on the future prospects and potential of NGOs in addressing complex global challenges.

Historical Roots and Enduring Impact of NGOs in Global Governance

In today's complex international order, the influence of nongovernmental organizations (NGOs) remains one of the clearest examples of how civil society shapes global governance beyond the authority of states. While it has become commonplace to claim that the significance of NGOs rose sharply after the Cold War, the truth is that NGOs have always played pivotal roles in global political life, often shaping international norms well before governments acted. Henri Dunant's response to the suffering he witnessed at the Battle of Solferino in 1859 led to the creation of the International Committee of the Red Cross and the adoption of the first Geneva Convention in 1864. This was more than an act of moral outrage, it was a landmark moment that gave birth to modern international humanitarian law—a legal and moral framework that remains vital today.

Such examples remind us that NGOs have historically been the catalysts for transnational change, often preceding the formal architecture of intergovernmental cooperation. The abolitionist movements that fought to end the slave trade, the suffrage campaigns that advanced women's political rights, and the anti-apartheid networks that brought global solidarity to the struggle in South Africa were all driven by voluntary associations operating beyond borders. These movements demonstrate that global civil society is not a new invention but an evolving force, adapting to technological, political, and cultural transformations.

The Digital Revolution and the Democratization of Civil Action

One of the most striking transformations in recent decades has been the digital revolution. In the popular imagination, the Internet is often seen as a top-down product of Cold War military research. Yet the truth is more nuanced: the first global NGO electronic networks in the 1980s and early 1990s were the quiet work of activists who realized that digital tools could break the barriers of distance and cost. The International Coalition for Development Action's Interdoc network, PeaceNet, GreenNet, and the Association for Progressive Communications were pioneers in building the digital backbone for global civil society. Long before social media became mainstream, these early networks linked grassroots groups across continents, giving them direct access to information, coordination, and advocacy channels that were previously unimaginable.

This democratization of communication remains one of the most profound advantages for NGOs today. Activists from remote villages to urban centers can now mobilize support, build coalitions, and pressure governments in real time. The global campaign by peasants in the Narmada Valley to halt World Bank funding for a dam project is a vivid example: local communities leveraged digital platforms to reach international audiences, demonstrating how marginalized voices can challenge powerful institutions when they have access to global networks.

Yet, while technology empowers, it also exposes civil society to new vulnerabilities. Authoritarian regimes have learned to exploit the same digital channels to monitor dissent, disrupt organizing, and spread disinformation. The Arab Spring was hailed as a triumph of online mobilization, but the same platforms have since been used to suppress protests and surveil activists. The balance between digital empowerment and digital repression is now one of the defining battlegrounds for NGOs.

NGOs and the United Nations: From Consultation to Influence

The relationship between NGOs and intergovernmental institutions such as the

United Nations illustrates both the promise and the limits of civil society's influence. When the U.N. Charter was drafted in San Francisco in 1945, NGOs successfully pressed delegates to enshrine principles of human rights and social justice. More importantly, they secured Article 71, which granted NGOs consultative status with the Economic and Social Council (ECOSOC). From this modest foothold, NGOs have expanded their presence dramatically. Today, more than 3,400 NGOs are recognized by the U.N., with rights to distribute documents, lobby delegates, organize side events, and even address official sessions.

Over time, NGOs have moved from the margins to the center of U.N. activities in areas such as human rights, women's empowerment, development, and environmental governance. Landmark treaties like the Convention on the Rights of the Child, the Ottawa Treaty banning landmines, and the International Criminal Court Statute were shaped by NGO coalitions that drafted proposals, lobbied states, and mobilized public opinion. In these cases, NGOs proved that they can be both advocates and technical experts, often bridging gaps in capacity that governments cannot fill alone.

However, gaining a seat at the table does not guarantee change on the ground. Many governments sign treaties or endorse ambitious declarations only to ignore them later, constrained by domestic opposition, lack of resources, or sheer inertia. NGOs have responded by evolving from policy lobbyists into watchdogs and implementation monitors. By producing parallel reports, generating media scrutiny, and pushing governments to honor their promises, NGOs keep international commitments alive long after the ink dries on official documents.

The tension between states and NGOs remains visible in the places where sovereignty is jealously guarded. The U.N. Security Council, the World Trade Organization, and international financial institutions like the IMF and World Bank grant NGOs no formal decision-making power. Yet even in these arenas, informal pathways exist—quiet consultations, expert briefings, and public campaigns that shape how debates unfold. In human rights, the breakthrough came when Amnesty International's relentless campaign against torture led to the 1984 Convention against Torture, marking a bold challenge to the principle of absolute state sovereignty. The creation of the International Criminal Court further institutionalized the idea that certain crimes are so grave that they transcend national jurisdiction—a concept propelled by NGO advocacy.

Accountability, Legitimacy, and the Democratic Contribution of NGOs

Critics often claim that NGOs lack democratic legitimacy. They point out, rightly, that many NGOs are small, self-selecting, and do not speak for majorities. Organizations like Greenpeace or Oxfam may not have formal memberships, while professional or faith-based NGOs derive legitimacy from expertise or moral standing rather than electoral representation. Proposals for a global "People's Assembly" have been floated to inject a democratic element into global governance, but practical barriers make this unlikely. Instead, NGOs enhance democracy in other ways: they increase transparency by bringing information into the public domain and expand debate by ensuring that marginalized perspectives are heard.

This dual role—information broker and advocate—makes NGOs indispensable in an age when policymaking is increasingly complex, technical, and distant from everyday citizens. In climate policy, for instance, NGOs help translate scientific data into public campaigns that push governments toward action. In labor rights, they expose abuses that corporations prefer to keep hidden. In public health, they mobilize communities during crises, as seen during the COVID-19 pandemic when civil society groups distributed protective equipment, countered misinformation, and pushed for equitable vaccine access.

Challenges Ahead: Civic Space, Strategic Alliances, and Moral Leadership

The future of global governance will test civil society's resilience and relevance. As geopolitical tensions sharpen, some states are closing civic space, restricting foreign funding, and labeling dissenting groups as "foreign agents." Simultaneously, new forms of civic engagement are emerging: decentralized youth movements, online activist collectives, and local mutual aid networks that defy traditional hierarchies. These grassroots energies challenge established NGOs to evolve—to become more representative, more transparent, and more agile.

At the same time, NGOs must navigate complex partnerships with businesses and states. Collaboration with corporations can amplify impact but also risks co-optation. Engagement with governments can secure policy wins but may blur the line between independence and complicity. The credibility of NGOs depends on their ability to maintain critical distance while forging pragmatic alliances.

In the end, the enduring power of NGOs does not lie in their formal authority but in their moral claim: the belief that ordinary people can come together, across borders and differences, to demand a fairer, safer, and more sustainable world. This belief is not naïve; it is rooted in centuries of hard-won victories—from the Red Cross and Geneva Conventions to the global campaigns against apartheid, landmines, and climate inaction.

As the challenges of the 21st century grow more interconnected—whether in the form of pandemics, cyber threats, or ecological collapse—civil society's role as both conscience and catalyst for global governance will remain vital. NGOs remind us that real change often begins not with governments but with citizens who refuse to accept the status quo. They hold power to account, amplify forgotten voices, and keep alive the radical idea that another world is not only possible but necessary.

If the story of global governance today is about balancing state sovereignty with global responsibility, then the story of NGOs is about ensuring that responsibility is not just negotiated behind closed doors but debated openly, shaped collectively, and defended relentlessly by those who dare to care. It is this restless, principled insistence on transparency, participation, and justice that keeps global governance from becoming merely technocratic—and keeps alive the promise of a global community bound not just by trade and treaties, but by solidarity and shared purpose.

Related Article to Read:

Erasmus, C.-L., & Glencorse, B. (2025, February 24). Why businesses must step up to sustain global civil society. World Economic Forum. https://www.weforum.org/stories/2025/02/why-businesses-sustain-global-civil-society/

➲ Key Summary

In "Why Businesses Must Step Up to Sustain Global Civil Society," Erasmus and Glencorse emphasize that businesses today have an urgent responsibility to help protect and strengthen the global civil society ecosystem. They argue that the social and political environment in which businesses operate is under threat from multiple directions—shrinking civic space, rising authoritarianism, deepening inequalities, and a backlash against human rights and democratic norms. Far from being separate from business interests, a thriving civil society is described as an essential condition for sustainable markets, stable investment environments, and innovation. The authors show how businesses benefit directly from societies where the rule of law, press freedom, community trust, and participatory governance are strong—conditions that civil society organizations, NGOs, community groups, and grassroots networks help to uphold every day.

The article highlights concrete ways in which the private sector can become a more active ally of civil society rather than merely a passive beneficiary. Businesses have resources, platforms, and influence that can protect civic space under threat, amplify marginalized voices, and defend the fundamental freedoms that enable open debate, advocacy, and accountability. For example, companies can speak out publicly when governments restrict free speech or repress activists, and they can leverage their economic power to push back against restrictive laws or corruption. They can also fund local initiatives, strengthen partnerships with grassroots organizations, and provide practical support such as technology, training, or safe meeting spaces. This proactive engagement is framed not as charity or corporate social responsibility alone, but as a strategic investment in resilient communities and stable operating environments.

Erasmus and Glencorse also caution that businesses should avoid selective engagement or 'purpose-washing'—where companies make grand statements about values while ignoring abuses or continuing to profit from contexts where civic freedoms are suppressed. Instead, the article calls for credible, consistent action that aligns business operations with the principles of open societies. This means respecting labor rights and fair taxation, ensuring supply chains do not harm communities, and championing diversity, inclusion, and human rights wherever they operate.

The authors stress that the challenges facing civil society today are too large and complex for NGOs to handle alone. The COVID-19 pandemic and new geopolitical tensions have made clear that collective action—across sectors and borders—is vital to respond to global crises and rebuild trust in democratic systems. When businesses join civil society and governments in genuine partnership, they help build resilient societies that are better equipped to tackle issues like corruption, climate change, inequality, and social division.

The piece concludes by urging companies to see civil society not as a compliance problem or reputational risk, but as a core partner in shaping the future of sustainable development, fair governance, and long-term prosperity. By stepping up as defenders of civic space and co-creators of just, inclusive societies, businesses not only protect their own social license to operate—they help ensure that democratic freedoms and community resilience can survive and thrive for generations to come.

➔ Key Insights

- Aid dependency creates systemic vulnerability: The decline in government aid creates wide-reaching socioeconomic instability—affecting both communities and corporate partners.
- Civic ecosystem as infrastructure: NGOs and community groups underpin legal frameworks, innovation, workforce development, and market trust—key to business viability.
- Business as civic stewards: Companies can fill the void through blended finance, impact investing, and civic bonds to sustain social and ecological services.
- Collaborative funding ecosystems: Proposals include multilateral funds (e.g., a "people and planet" fund) and partnerships that bring together business, NGOs, governments, and diaspora investors.
- Strategic CSR beyond optics: The role of CSR should transform from branding to active participation in civic resilience and public infrastructure support. opportunities for more diverse leadership and friction over fair representation.

Discussion Questions

1. Why is it important to recognize that NGOs have shaped global norms long before the end of the Cold War?
2. How did early NGO pioneers influence the development of the Internet for civil society use?
3. In what ways do NGOs enhance democracy in global governance despite lacking formal representation?
4. How do NGOs navigate the tension between maintaining independence and partnering with states or corporations?
5. What lessons can be drawn from the successes and limits of NGOs' influence in areas like human rights or environmental policy?
6. What challenges might future generations of NGOs face in a digital but increasingly authoritarian global context?

Key Terms and Concepts

Nongovernmental Organizations (NGOs) – Voluntary associations independent of governments that pursue policy goals, provide services, and mobilize public support.

Global Civil Society – The transnational sphere of citizen action and organization that operates beyond the nation-state.

Geneva Convention – International treaties establishing standards for humanitarian treatment in war, initiated by the Red Cross.

Interdoc, PeaceNet, GreenNet, APC – Early examples of NGO-driven global electronic networks.

Consultative Status (ECOSOC) – Official recognition allowing NGOs to participate in U.N. activities.

Watchdog Function – The role of NGOs in monitoring governments to ensure they implement international commitments.

Sovereignty Barrier – The principle that domestic affairs are shielded from external interference, historically challenged by human rights campaigns.

International Criminal Court (ICC) – A permanent tribunal for prosecuting war crimes and crimes against humanity, supported by global NGO coalitions.

People's Assembly – A proposed but unrealized idea for a democratic global parliamentary body to complement the U.N. General Assembly.

Major Groups – Stakeholder categories recognized in global environmental governance to structure NGO participation.

Learning Objectives

By the end of this chapter, students will be able to:

- Explain how NGOs have historically shaped global governance and international norms.
- Analyze the structural inequalities that influence which NGOs gain access and authority in international institutions.
- Discuss the double-edged role of technology for civil society mobilization and state surveillance.
- Evaluate tensions between NGO professionalization and grassroots legitimacy.
- Assess how NGOs contribute to achieving global goals like the SDGs while navigating insider–outsider dynamics.
- Reflect on the continuing challenges NGOs face in balancing independence, funding, accountability, and impact.

Persistent Inequalities in Global Governance Architecture

Yet even as NGOs have carved out this multifaceted role—insider advocates, watchdogs, norm-setters, and grassroots mobilizers—they continue to navigate persistent structural inequalities within the very architecture of global governance. For all the formal spaces where civil society is welcomed, significant asymmetries remain. As Tallberg et al. (2013) remind us, "international organizations have become more open to nonstate actors, but this openness is neither uniform nor unconditional" (p. 4). Access varies by issue area, by region, and by the historical legacy of the organization in question. Climate negotiations, for example, have seen extensive civil society involvement compared to security forums like the UN Security Council, which remains almost entirely the domain of states.

Moreover, even within relatively open arenas like human rights, the kinds of NGOs that secure consistent influence often share similar traits: they are large, professionally run, fluent in the procedural language of diplomacy, and well-connected to donor networks in the Global North. This structural bias risks reproducing an echo chamber in which local, indigenous, or small-scale voices—particularly from the Global South—struggle to gain visibility and resources. As Stroup and Wong (2017) argue, "NGOs can fall into an authority trap, where the very structures that give them credibility in global fora also distance them from the grassroots they claim to represent" (p. 3).

Strategies for Inclusion: Coalition-Building and Digital Advocacy

To address this gap, new forms of coalition building and networked advocacy have emerged. Transnational issue networks often link global NGOs with local partners who bring lived experience and context-specific expertise. For instance, campaigns for land rights, indigenous sovereignty, or gender justice increasingly emphasize partnerships that share decision-making power and amplify frontline leadership. These alliances remind us that civil society's power does not reside solely in polished headquarters but also in the solidarity ties that connect local struggles to international audiences.

Technology plays a double-edged role here. On one hand, digital platforms have dramatically lowered the barriers for marginalized communities to tell their own stories, mobilize supporters, and bypass traditional gatekeepers. Social media campaigns—whether for environmental defenders in the Amazon or youth climate strikes inspired by Greta Thunberg—demonstrate how quickly grassroots voices can leap into global consciousness. On the other hand, the same technologies expose activists to surveillance, online harassment, and state censorship. The closure of civic space online is now recognized by the UN as one of the defining challenges for civil society in the 21st century.

Trust, Legitimacy, and the Risks of Professionalization

Within this environment, NGOs must also grapple with the changing nature of public trust. As Stroup and Wong (2017) explain, "the expansion of NGO authority has not been matched by parallel innovations in accountability" (p. 5). Skepticism toward global elites—fueled by populist movements in many countries—often extends to international NGOs, which are portrayed by critics as out-of-touch or beholden to foreign interests. High-profile scandals or governance failures, even if isolated, can fuel narratives that question the integrity of the sector as a whole. In response, many NGOs have doubled down on transparency initiatives, participatory governance models, and efforts to demonstrate tangible impact.

Yet this professionalization has unintended consequences. As NGOs adopt business-like performance metrics and branding strategies, some fear they risk losing the radical edge that once set them apart from states and markets. Critics argue that civil society's unique value lies in its capacity to disrupt, to imagine alternatives, and to demand accountability in ways that technocratic management tools alone cannot deliver. As Ruhlman (2020) cautions, "the legitimacy of NGOs is ultimately relational and contingent—it rests not just on efficiency but on trust, shared norms, and the moral force of collective action" (p. 9).

Hybrid Roles in Complex Governance Systems

These tensions are not new. From their earliest incarnations—the abolitionists, the suffragettes, the peace leagues—civil society movements have always balanced insider influence with outsider pressure, institutional engagement with street-level protest. What is striking today is how this balancing act plays out on a truly global scale. As governance becomes more complex and polycentric—spanning states, intergovernmental bodies, corporations, and informal networks—the places where NGOs can insert themselves multiply, but so too do the expectations they must meet.

An illustrative example can be seen in the Sustainable Development Goals (SDGs). Unlike the Millennium Development Goals before them, the SDGs were explicitly designed to include multi-stakeholder partnerships. NGOs were deeply involved in the consultation process that shaped the goals and now play critical roles in implementation, monitoring, and public awareness. Yet this also places them under constant pressure to deliver, to coordinate with governments and businesses, and to negotiate the trade-offs that arise when global ambitions meet local realities.

Beyond global summits and frameworks, the everyday work of NGOs also remains rooted in contexts where governance is fragile or contested. In conflict zones, humanitarian NGOs provide life-saving assistance where states are unwilling or unable to act. In authoritarian settings, human rights defenders document abuses and support local activists despite severe risks. In climate justice campaigns, indigenous organizations lead resistance to extractive industries threatening ancestral lands. In each case, the lines between service provision, advocacy, and direct action blur—revealing the hybrid nature of modern NGOs as both partners and challengers of state power.

Scholars now speak of a "double movement" in global civil society: one part professionalized, networked, and embedded in formal institutions; another part horizontal, decentralized, and insurgent—often using new digital tactics to outmaneuver censorship and repression. This double movement reflects an enduring truth: NGOs are not monolithic. They range from huge international bureaucracies to small, community-based initiatives; from legally registered charities to loose activist collectives. This diversity is a source of resilience, but also of fragmentation and uneven capacity.

Navigating Contradictions: The Future of NGO Engagement

As the landscape evolves, the questions that preoccupy researchers and practitioners alike remain remarkably consistent: How can NGOs maintain independence while securing sustainable funding? How can they amplify marginalized voices without appropriating them? How can they push global governance to be more inclusive while avoiding co-optation or mission drift? And how can they balance urgency—responding to crises in real time—with the slow work of building durable institutions and norms?

In the final analysis, the continued relevance of NGOs in global governance depends on their ability to inhabit these contradictions productively. Their greatest strength may lie not in offering definitive solutions, but in embodying a form of politics that is at once local and global, pragmatic and visionary, grounded in communities yet capable of shifting international agendas. In the words of Ruhlman (2020), "NGOs remind us that governance beyond the state is a living practice—imperfect, contested, and essential."

If we accept that no single actor—whether state, market, or civil society—can alone address the complex, interdependent crises of our century, then the question becomes not whether NGOs matter, but how they can best contribute. That question calls for continued research, reflection, and above all, the active participation of those whose lives global governance aims to improve.

Related Article to Read:

FundsforNGOs. (n.d.). The importance of NGO accreditation with the United Nations. FundsforNGOs. Retrieved from https://www2.fundsforngos.org/articles/the-importance-of-ngo-accreditation-with-the-united-nations/

Key Summary

UN Accreditation, especially through consultative status with the United Nations Economic and Social Council (ECOSOC), is a powerful milestone for any NGO aiming to influence global policy and participate in multilateral dialogue. This status is not merely symbolic—it formally recognizes an NGO's credibility, transparency, and operational maturity and grants it access to decision-making spaces at the UN that are otherwise reserved for member states and intergovernmental actors.

The article explains that consultative status allows NGOs to attend UN conferences, participate in international meetings, submit written statements, deliver oral interventions, and even organize side-events that can shape policy discussions and global agendas. For many NGOs, this access creates opportunities to build alliances with governments, lobby for policy changes, and raise awareness for issues that might otherwise be ignored on the international stage. This has been critical for amplifying voices on human rights, environmental protection, gender equality, and other transnational concerns.

However, securing accreditation is far from automatic. The UN Committee on NGOs under ECOSOC reviews each application rigorously, assessing the organization's governance, transparency, impact, and alignment with the UN Charter's principles. An NGO must demonstrate a minimum of two years of active operations and submit detailed documentation proving its legitimacy and track record. This vetting process is intended to maintain the credibility of civil society representation within the UN.

Yet, the article highlights that the system is not without flaws. While the accreditation framework is designed to encourage broad participation, the approval process can be highly politicized. Powerful member states sitting on the ECOSOC Committee can block or delay applications from NGOs whose missions they view as politically sensitive or threatening. Human rights and democracy advocacy groups often face extra scrutiny or obstacles, especially when their work challenges the interests of authoritarian regimes. As a result, some credible organizations are denied access, which undermines the UN's commitment to inclusive dialogue.

Another insight is that accredited NGOs need more than just the status itself—they must know how to use it strategically. Many small or grassroots groups lack the resources or institutional capacity to maintain a consistent presence at UN headquarters in New York or Geneva, and the day-to-day work of monitoring UN agendas, attending meetings, and building coalitions requires time and expertise. Thus, while accreditation opens doors, it does not guarantee influence unless NGOs have a clear plan for engagement and the networks to back their advocacy.

Finally, the summary underscores that accreditation can enhance an NGO's standing with donors, governments, and other partners. Being able to say that an organization holds consultative status signals legitimacy, accountability, and the capacity to operate on a global scale—qualities that can strengthen funding applications and partnership opportunities.

In sum, the article presents accreditation not just as an administrative step, but as a strategic tool for amplifying civil society's role in global governance—while also warning that NGOs must navigate its bureaucratic and political complexities with careful planning, coalition building, and resilience.

➔ Key Insights

- Accreditation offers both prestige and practical access—unprecedented opportunities to influence global policy and engage in diplomatic forums.
- The application process is technical but deeply political; representation on the ECOSOC committee often reflects geopolitical divides.
- This creates an uneven playing field: organizations from repressive or less influential states sometimes struggle to be recognized.
- Knowledge of UN accreditation systems (e.g., iCSO/ESANGO) is vital for NGOs to plan strategic engagement with global governance.

Discussion Questions

1. According to Tallberg et al. (2013), how does access to international organizations vary for NGOs? Give examples.
2. What do Stroup and Wong (2017) mean by the "authority trap," and how does it affect local voices?
3. How has digital technology empowered and endangered civil society actors simultaneously?
4. In what ways does NGO professionalization create new risks for their legitimacy?
5. Discuss the role of NGOs in implementing and monitoring the Sustainable Development Goals. What tensions arise?
6. How can NGOs balance insider influence and outsider activism in global governance?
7. Reflect on Ruhlman's (2020) point that "the legitimacy of NGOs is ultimately relational and contingent." What does this imply for their future?

Key Terms and Concepts

NGO Authority Trap – The risk that organizational structures which grant NGOs influence also distance them from grassroots connections.

Civic Space – The political and digital environments that allow civil society to operate freely.

Insider–Outsider Dynamics – The balancing act NGOs perform between engaging institutions and mobilizing grassroots action.

Transnational Advocacy Networks – Cross-border coalitions linking local and international civil society actors.

SDGs (Sustainable Development Goals) – The global framework involving governments, businesses, and NGOs to address key development challenges.

Digital Mobilization – The use of social media and online platforms for rapid organizing, fundraising, and campaigning.

Professionalization of NGOs – The trend toward business-like practices, performance metrics, and branding in the nonprofit sector.

Global Governance – The systems of rules, institutions, and networks through which global affairs are managed beyond state actors.

Reference

Stroup, S. S., & Wong, W. H. (2017). *The Authority Trap: Strategic Choices of International NGOs.* Cornell University Press.

Tallberg, J., Sommerer, T., Squatrito, T., & Jönsson, C. (2013). *The Opening Up of International Organizations: Transnational Access in Global Governance.* Cambridge University Press.

Ruhlman, S. (2020). *NGOs and the Authority of Civil Society: Collective Action in an Era of Accountability*. Routledge.

Learning Objectives

By the end of this chapter, students will be able to:

- Explain how NGOs have historically shaped global governance and international norms.
- Analyze the structural inequalities that influence which NGOs gain access and authority in international institutions.
- Discuss the double-edged role of technology for civil society mobilization and state surveillance.
- Evaluate tensions between NGO professionalization and grassroots legitimacy.
- Assess how NGOs contribute to achieving global goals like the SDGs while navigating insider–outsider dynamics.
- Reflect on the continuing challenges NGOs face in balancing independence, funding, accountability, and impact.

From Philanthropy to Strategy: The Expanding Role of CSR

Corporate Social Responsibility (CSR) has evolved far beyond the early days of industrial philanthropy, when wealthy business leaders funded libraries or hospitals to enhance their reputations. In today's deeply interconnected global economy, CSR has become a core element of business strategy and reputation management. It responds to rising public expectations that companies must not only generate profit but also contribute meaningfully to social welfare, environmental stewardship, and sustainable development. This expansion of corporate responsibility is shaped by multiple pressures: tighter regulatory frameworks, activist shareholders, empowered consumers, and perhaps most significantly, the increasingly organized voice of civil society.

NGOs as Essential Partners: Legitimacy, Trust, and Accountability

In this dynamic landscape, NGOs play a critical role as catalysts, watchdogs, and bridge-builders. They provide a unique kind of legitimacy that companies alone rarely possess. Local communities may distrust the intentions of large corporations, particularly in regions where resource extraction, industrial pollution, or exploitative labor practices have caused lasting harm. NGOs often fill this trust gap because they are embedded in local contexts, speak the language of rights and responsibilities, and can connect community perspectives to national and global audiences.

It is not just a question of who delivers services but of how trust is built and sustained. NGOs bring knowledge of local needs, cultural sensitivities, and the kinds of community engagement that are essential for CSR projects to succeed. This is particularly important in sectors like mining, energy, agriculture, and manufacturing, where corporate activities directly affect livelihoods and the environment. When properly designed, cross-sector partnerships allow corporations to demonstrate that they are not merely extracting profit but investing in the communities and ecosystems that sustain their operations.

Moldovan et al. (2016) point out that CSR, when pursued through genuine partnerships with civil society, complements the role of the state in delivering social goods, rather than replacing it (p. 55). This perspective challenges the tendency of some companies to view CSR as a public relations tool or as a substitute for fair regulation and taxation. True partnership means shared accountability, participatory governance, and mutual benefit—not just branding exercises or token donations.

The stakes are high. Global supply chains have connected consumers in the Global North with factories, farms, and mines in the Global South, where working conditions often escape robust oversight. NGOs have exposed dangerous working environments, child labor, and other abuses that companies either failed to monitor or deliberately overlooked. These revelations have driven international campaigns, consumer boycotts, and regulatory changes that forced companies to take responsibility for the entire value chain, not just the final product. It was not corporate boards alone that created fair trade labels, sweatshop monitoring, or conflict mineral disclosures—it was NGOs, labor unions, and community groups pushing relentlessly for ethical standards.

This history illustrates that CSR is rarely voluntary in practice. Companies adapt because stakeholders—workers, communities, investors, governments—demand it. NGOs are key to transforming these demands into sustained pressure and practical guidance. For example, when global apparel brands signed the Bangladesh Accord on Fire and Building Safety after the Rana Plaza disaster in 2013, it was not out of pure goodwill but because NGOs, trade unions, and media scrutiny forced corporate leaders to acknowledge their responsibilities and implement binding safety standards.

Balancing Power: Risks and Innovations in NGO-Corporate Partnerships

Yet the relationship between NGOs and corporations is not just adversarial. Many modern CSR initiatives are co-designed by companies and NGOs that see mutual benefit in aligning business success with social progress. In the food and beverage industry, large companies have partnered with environmental NGOs to protect water sources, promote sustainable agriculture, or support climate resilience in rural communities. In extractive industries, community development projects often involve NGOs to ensure local participation and conflict mediation. Such collaboration can help companies secure what is often called a "social license to operate"—the informal acceptance by local stakeholders that the company's presence brings net benefits.

But partnership also comes with risks. NGOs must safeguard their independence and avoid being co-opted by corporate funding. Moldovan et al. (2016) caution that "CSR partnerships should not become a mechanism to privatize public goods without democratic control" (p. 56). When corporations dominate the agenda, there is a danger that community needs become secondary to brand image or investor relations. Furthermore, NGOs risk losing credibility if they are perceived as too close to corporate partners, particularly when they are dependent on corporate grants for survival.

This tension has driven a shift toward more formal frameworks for partnership governance. Many NGOs now insist on clear memoranda of understanding that outline roles, responsibilities, conflict resolution mechanisms, and community accountability structures. Some CSR partnerships are shaped by multi-stakeholder initiatives that bring together businesses, NGOs, governments, and community representatives to co-create solutions. These arrangements can strengthen legitimacy by ensuring that corporate investments reflect genuine local priorities rather than top-down corporate agendas.

Technology and Governance: Tools, Transparency, and Public Policy

Technology has transformed this landscape. Digital tools enable NGOs to monitor corporate behavior more systematically, from satellite imagery of deforestation to real-time reporting of labor abuses through mobile apps. Social media has amplified the voices of affected communities and made reputational risks immediate and global. Companies that fail to deliver on CSR commitments can face viral backlash that erodes brand value overnight. Conversely, technology has also given corporations and NGOs new ways to collaborate, share data, and scale impact. Open data platforms, online stakeholder consultations, and blockchain for supply chain transparency are just a few examples of innovations that blend technological efficiency with ethical oversight.

The professionalization of both CSR and NGOs adds another layer of complexity. Large NGOs increasingly recruit staff with corporate experience, management training, and technical expertise in impact measurement. This has improved the rigor of CSR project design and evaluation but also blurs the lines between civil society and business. Some critics worry that when NGOs become too "corporate," they lose their grassroots connection and moral authority. The challenge is to maintain a clear sense of mission and values while embracing the tools and language needed to operate in a highly competitive funding environment.

Meanwhile, the state still matters. Governments set the legal frameworks within which CSR operates, from mandatory reporting requirements to tax incentives for social investment. Public policy can either strengthen or weaken the conditions that make meaningful CSR possible. In some countries, weak governance or corruption can make it tempting for companies to substitute token CSR for compliance with labor laws, environmental regulations, or fair taxation. Here, NGOs play an important watchdog role, ensuring that CSR is not a smokescreen for deregulation but a complement to effective governance.

Toward Shared Value: Future Directions for CSR and Civil Society

Looking ahead, the future of CSR and NGO partnerships will be shaped by major global challenges. Climate change, for example, demands cross-sector collaboration at an unprecedented scale. The transition to sustainable energy, circular production models, and climate resilience requires companies to rethink their entire business models and supply chains. NGOs are essential partners in this transition, bringing technical expertise, local knowledge, and public trust to projects that must align global ambition with community realities.

Similarly, the Sustainable Development Goals (SDGs) have made it clear that private capital must play a role in financing development priorities, but civil society must ensure that this role does not replace public accountability. From fair wages and decent work to gender equality and biodiversity, NGOs hold companies to account for contributing real value—not just symbolic gestures—to the global public good.

Students of global governance should understand that CSR is not just an optional add-on for corporations but an evolving practice shaped by shifting norms, stakeholder pressure, and collaborative problem-solving. NGOs stand at the heart of this practice—as critics, partners, co-creators, and conscience-keepers.

In the final analysis, meaningful CSR depends on shared responsibility. Companies must be willing to embed sustainability and ethics at the core of their operations. NGOs must balance their independence with strategic engagement that can scale impact. Communities must have real voice and agency to define what "responsibility" means in their context. And governments must craft and enforce policies that make doing the right thing the norm, not the exception.

This intricate balance holds the promise that profit and purpose do not need to be in conflict. When NGOs and corporations navigate this relationship with transparency, mutual respect, and commitment to the common good, CSR becomes more than a slogan—it becomes a pathway to shared value and resilient societies in a world that demands new models of cooperation and accountability.

Related Article to Read:

FundsforNGOs. (n.d.). The best case studies of cross-sector partnerships for NGO funding. FundsforNGOs. Retrieved from https://www2.fundsforngos.org/articles-searching-grants-and-donors/the-best-case-studies-of-cross-sector-partnerships-for-ngo-funding/

➔ Key Summary

This article from FundsforNGOs explores how innovative cross-sector partnerships have emerged as one of the most resilient and impactful strategies for NGOs to secure funding, scale their programs, and create sustainable social change. Instead of depending solely on traditional grants or donations, NGOs are increasingly building alliances with corporations, governments, foundations, and other non-state actors to address complex global challenges that no single sector can solve alone.

The text examines real-world cases to show how diverse organizations—from local community-based groups to large international NGOs—have leveraged such partnerships to access new resources, expand technical capacity, and gain legitimacy in the eyes of multiple stakeholders. For example, the Emergency Capacity Building (ECB) Project stands out as a landmark collaboration. Launched in the early 2000s by a consortium of major humanitarian NGOs like CARE, Save the Children, and Oxfam, and funded by donors such as the Bill & Melinda Gates Foundation and ECHO, the ECB Project aimed to strengthen emergency response capacity through shared training, joint field operations, and common standards. This pooled effort enabled participating organizations to respond faster and more effectively to disasters in dozens of countries.

Another significant case study is the Partnership for Refugees, initiated during the Obama administration. Facing unprecedented refugee flows, this initiative mobilized leading tech companies, multinationals, and social enterprises—including Airbnb,

Google, HP, and Microsoft—to pledge financial resources, technological solutions, and employment pathways for displaced communities worldwide. The partnership showcased how corporate assets, like digital infrastructure and hiring networks, could be aligned with civil society's on-the-ground knowledge to tackle humanitarian crises more holistically.

The article also references smaller, region-specific examples, such as recycling and environmental sustainability collaborations in Southeast Asia. In Indonesia, for instance, local NGOs have worked with beverage companies like PT Aqua Golden Mississippi (Danone Indonesia) to develop community-based waste collection systems that support informal waste pickers while meeting corporate sustainability goals. These grassroots-oriented partnerships not only advance environmental impact but also demonstrate how local legitimacy and cultural sensitivity can strengthen CSR outcomes.

What ties these diverse examples together is a recognition that effective partnerships are rarely quick-fix CSR add-ons. Instead, they require shared governance, mutual accountability, and robust community engagement mechanisms. Successful alliances are built on clear agreements that define roles, responsibilities, and conflict resolution processes. They emphasize co-creation rather than top-down implementation, allowing community voices to shape priorities and ensure that corporate contributions do not overshadow local needs.

The article further explains that such collaborations are not without risks. When NGOs become overly dependent on corporate funding, they may face pressure to align too closely with business interests, risking mission drift or reputational harm. To mitigate this, many leading NGOs insist on formal memoranda of understanding, transparent reporting, and participatory evaluation frameworks that protect their independence while maximizing shared value.

Another critical insight is that strong cross-sector partnerships often invest in capacity building for local stakeholders. Instead of treating NGOs as mere service providers, companies and funders that prioritize community leadership help build long-term resilience. This approach shifts the dynamic from one-off donations to true partnerships where knowledge, risks, and benefits are shared.

Ultimately, the article positions these case studies as living proof that when designed with intention, cross-sector partnerships can transform how development goals are funded and delivered. They blur the traditional lines between business, philanthropy, and civil society, unlocking solutions that neither side could achieve alone.

➔ Key Insights

- Cross-sector partnerships amplify impact by combining resources and expertise while fostering innovation.
- High-impact models, such as the ECB Project and refugee private-sector engagement, show that joint efforts can yield scalable, multi-country programs.
- Successful collaborations hinge on transparent governance and shared decision-making.
- Local NGO involvement ensures cultural relevance and community trust.
- Even after crises, partnerships can deepen—with funders improving oversight without abandoning cooperation

Discussion Questions

1. Why is it important for companies to partner with NGOs rather than pursuing CSR initiatives alone?
2. How does technology simultaneously strengthen and complicate NGO–corporate partnerships?
3. In what ways can CSR partnerships risk undermining NGO independence or community priorities?
4. Why do some scholars argue that CSR is rarely truly "voluntary"?
5. How can formal governance frameworks help balance power between corporations and NGOs in partnerships?
6. Discuss an example where digital tools have enhanced transparency and accountability in global supply chains.
7. How do governments shape the incentives and limits of CSR, and what role do NGOs play in this context?
8. Why is community trust a critical factor in the success of CSR projects?
9. How can NGOs maintain their grassroots legitimacy while engaging in complex cross-sector collaborations?
10. How do CSR initiatives contribute to achieving the Sustainable Development Goals (SDGs)?

Key Terms and Concepts

Corporate Social Responsibility (CSR) – Corporate practices and strategies that aim to align business operations with social, environmental, and ethical responsibilities.

Cross-Sector Partnerships – Collaborations between NGOs, corporations, governments, and communities to achieve shared social or environmental objectives.

Social License to Operate – The informal acceptance by local stakeholders that a company's operations are legitimate and beneficial to the community.

Stakeholder Accountability – The obligation to be transparent and responsive to those affected by corporate or NGO activities.

Watchdog Role – The function of NGOs to monitor corporate behavior, expose abuses, and push for accountability.

Multi-Stakeholder Initiatives (MSIs) – Formal collaborations that bring together diverse actors—corporations, NGOs, governments, communities—to co-design solutions to complex problems.

Professionalization – The trend toward hiring staff with corporate or technical expertise in NGOs, often to manage complex projects or measure impact.

Digital Transparency – Using digital tools to monitor, share, and verify information about corporate practices and supply chains.

Co-optation – The risk that NGOs lose independence or mission clarity when they rely too heavily on corporate funding or partnerships.

Sustainable Development Goals (SDGs) – The UN's global agenda for addressing social, economic, and environmental challenges by 2030.

Institutional Voids – Gaps where governments fail to deliver essential public goods, often filled by NGOs and private companies through partnerships.

Reference

Moldovan, O., Green, T., & Potcovaru, A.-M. (2016). Corporate Social Responsibility and Cross-Sector Partnerships: The Role of NGOs. *Romanian Economic and Business Review*, 11(3), 51–56.

Learning Objectives

By the end of this chapter, students will be able to:

- Explain the connection between civic space and digital rights in the 21st century.
- Analyze how digital technologies empower and threaten civil society.
- Identify key challenges such as surveillance, internet shutdowns, and algorithmic governance.
- Discuss the role of civil society in defending privacy, freedom of expression, and digital inclusion.
- Evaluate real-world cases that illustrate how digital rights shape civic participation globally.

The Digital Turn in Civic Space: Promise and Paradox

In the twenty-first century, the protection of civic space increasingly depends on how we understand and safeguard our digital rights. As more of social, political, and civic life shifts online, the internet has become not only a marketplace of ideas but also a contested arena where power, freedom, and control constantly collide. For civil society, this digital migration has opened unprecedented opportunities to connect, organize, and amplify marginalized voices—but it has also created new risks and vulnerabilities that test the very foundations of democratic participation.

The promise of digitalisation is visible in countless acts of everyday civic action. Community groups in remote villages use mobile messaging to coordinate disaster relief. Indigenous activists share live videos of land encroachments that once would have gone unnoticed. Human rights defenders document abuses and instantly distribute evidence to the world. Young people, inspired by global climate strikes or protests against systemic racism, mobilize millions through hashtags, memes, and viral campaigns. In these moments, the digital sphere feels like the ultimate equalizer: any individual, regardless of wealth or status, can find an audience, build solidarity, and challenge entrenched power.

Repression by Design: State and Corporate Control in the Digital Age

Yet alongside these promises is a stark reality. The same tools that connect can also control. The same networks that lift up local stories can also expose those telling them to surveillance, harassment, or violent reprisals. As Brot für die Welt (2022) warns, "The internet should guarantee freedom of expression worldwide, but today the opposite is true in many countries: it is the perfect tool for oppression" (p. 5). Authoritarian regimes have learned quickly that controlling the digital commons means controlling dissent itself. The proliferation of sophisticated spyware, data tracking tools, facial recognition systems, and vast biometric databases has created a landscape in which activists are watched, profiled, and targeted at a scale that was unthinkable a generation ago.

Internet shutdowns have become a blunt but effective weapon in the modern toolkit of digital repression. They are used to silence protestors, disrupt organizing, and cut citizens off from the rest of the world. In Myanmar, the military junta's repeated internet blackouts have aimed to weaken the resilience of a powerful civil resistance movement. In India, local shutdowns have become routine to stifle demonstrations or quell unrest, often justified under vague notions of public safety. Elsewhere, from Iran to Sudan to Ethiopia, entire regions have been thrown into digital darkness at moments when connection was most needed to hold power accountable.

Yet the erosion of civic space online is not only the work of oppressive states. It is also embedded in the business models of the world's most powerful corporations. The rise of surveillance capitalism means that vast amounts of personal information—our movements, preferences, contacts, and private communications—are harvested, traded, and analyzed for profit. As Brot für die Welt puts it, "Digital corporations gain enormous power from collecting vast amounts of data. This power is political as well as economic" (p. 20). Social media platforms and search engines, driven by algorithms optimized for engagement, amplify sensational and divisive content, feeding polarization and sometimes stoking violence. Civil society groups that once celebrated the democratizing power of digital tools now find themselves fighting to hold platforms accountable for spreading disinformation, hate speech, or propaganda that directly undermines their work.

This tension is compounded by the reality that many civic organizations rely on the very platforms that pose these risks. Messaging apps, cloud services, online fundraising tools, and social media have become essential to how NGOs and grassroots groups organize, communicate, and reach supporters. But each digital footprint carries the risk of surveillance—by hostile states, opportunistic criminals, or the platforms themselves. The paradox is clear: digitalisation empowers civil society while making it more vulnerable than ever before.

The Unequal Internet: Digital Divides and Democratic Exclusion

Beneath these global trends, deep inequalities shape who can participate meaningfully in digital civic space. The digital divide remains a stubborn barrier, separating the connected and the disconnected along lines of wealth, geography, gender, age, and language. In parts of the Global South, rural communities struggle with unreliable internet, high costs of devices, or limited digital literacy. People with disabilities often face platforms and tools that are inaccessible by design. Older generations or linguistic minorities may find global debates and online advocacy dominated by a narrow elite fluent in English and the codes of internet culture. As a result, while some voices grow louder, others risk being silenced not by censorship but by exclusion.

This divide was starkly visible during the COVID-19 pandemic. When lockdowns forced civil society organizations to shift meetings, protests, and services online, communities without stable connections or devices were effectively locked out of civic life. Digital exclusion, once seen as an economic issue, emerged clearly as a democratic one.

Digital Resistance: Civil Society Innovation and Legal Advocacy

Despite these challenges, civil society actors around the world continue to innovate to defend and expand digital rights. Grassroots groups and technologists build encrypted messaging apps, secure platforms for collaboration, and open-source tools adapted for low-bandwidth contexts. Digital security trainings have become vital for journalists, human rights defenders, and youth activists alike. Networks such as Access Now, Privacy International, and the Electronic Frontier Foundation fight for stronger data protection laws and challenge abusive surveillance in courts and legislatures. Strategic litigation has forced states and corporations to uphold privacy and freedom of expression, from India's Supreme Court ruling on privacy as a fundamental right to the EU's landmark General Data Protection Regulation (GDPR).

But protecting civic space online is not only a technical or legal question; it is also about building people's capacity to act. Digital literacy is fundamental. It means teaching communities how to protect their data, identify disinformation, demand accountability, and use technology to organize safely and effectively. This is where schools, libraries, universities, and local NGOs play a frontline role. Around the world, youth-led movements show how digital tools can be used not just for protest but for education, mutual aid, and community care. From feminist collectives in Latin America to climate networks in Europe and Africa, young people are weaving digital and offline strategies to claim space that is democratic and inclusive.

Algorithmic and Biometric Threats to Rights and Inclusion

Algorithmic governance adds another layer of complexity. Invisible algorithms decide which stories surface and which vanish, what content is labeled misinformation or hate speech, and whose voices are amplified or silenced. This power shapes public opinion, election outcomes, and civic debate. But it remains largely unregulated and opaque. Recent moves such as the European Union's Digital Services Act, which requires companies to explain how their algorithms shape information flows, show

how policy can respond to civil society's demand for transparency and accountability. Yet much remains to be done to ensure that algorithmic systems serve the public good rather than corporate profit alone.

Addressing the risks to civic space also requires confronting the spread of biometric surveillance. Many governments now use digital ID systems, facial recognition, and biometric databases in the name of efficiency or security. In practice, these tools often deepen inequality and erode privacy. India's Aadhaar system, Kenya's Huduma Namba, and China's vast surveillance grids raise urgent questions about consent, oversight, and discrimination. Marginalized communities—migrants, racial minorities, Indigenous groups—are often the first to bear the costs of misuse and the last to benefit from promised protections.

Shaping a Democratic Digital Future: Collective Responsibility and Civic Action

The good news is that civil society has proven resilient and adaptive. Coalitions of lawyers, technologists, journalists, and activists are challenging misuse of digital surveillance and winning important victories. Strategic alliances with ethical businesses and public interest technologists are creating alternative models for digital governance. Local communities are developing digital tools that respect cultural contexts, linguistic diversity, and collective ownership of data. These actions remind us that the shape of our digital future is not fixed but open to contestation and co-creation.

As Brot für die Welt reminds us, "It is up to us to shape digitalisation in a way that expands civic space rather than restricts it" (p. 6). Doing so demands clear-eyed recognition that technology alone will not protect rights. It requires states to uphold fundamental freedoms, companies to act with accountability, and citizens to organize, learn, and demand a seat at the table where digital futures are decided.

Protecting civic space and digital rights is thus not a luxury for advanced democracies alone—it is a frontline struggle everywhere that people gather, speak out, and work together for a better future. In the words of many digital rights advocates, the fight for a free, open, and inclusive internet is the fight for democracy itself.

Related Article to Read:

Paradigm Initiative. (2024, November 5). Press release: 12th edition of the Digital Rights and Inclusion Forum (DRIF25) launched with calls to guard the Internet as a civic space. DRIF. Retrieved from https://drif.paradigmhq.org/press-release-12th-edition-of-the-digital-rights-and-inclusion-forum-drif25-launched-with-calls-to-guard-the-internet-as-a-civic-space/

➔ Key Summary

The 12th edition of the Digital Rights and Inclusion Forum (DRIF), hosted by the Paradigm Initiative, has reaffirmed the urgent need to recognize the internet as a vital civic space—especially in regions where traditional civic spaces are under growing threat. Speaking in Lusaka, Zambia, Executive Director 'Gbenga Sesan emphasized that for many communities in the Global South, digital spaces have become the last remaining arena where citizens can freely assemble, express dissent, organize collectively, and hold power to account. This urgency stems from increasing trends across Africa where governments invoke broad notions of "national security" to pass restrictive laws, conduct mass surveillance, and implement internet shutdowns that directly curtail freedom of speech and democratic participation.

DRIF, which has evolved from its earlier form as the Internet Freedom Forum (IFF), has become an annual convening point that unites diverse actors—policy makers, human rights defenders, journalists, youth leaders, tech companies, and UN agencies—to debate how to safeguard human rights in a rapidly digitizing society. The forum provides a rare multi-stakeholder platform for bridging policy gaps and nurturing locally grounded solutions that respect African social contexts while addressing global standards for privacy, free expression, and equitable access. One of the highlights of this year's gathering is its theme of "Digital Ubuntu," an idea that draws from Africa's deep-rooted ethos of community interdependence and collective dignity. By applying Ubuntu to digital governance, DRIF25 hopes to reframe debates about privacy, surveillance, and inclusion in ways that avoid simply copying imported regulatory models and instead build frameworks that resonate with local values and communal solidarity.

The Paradigm Initiative and its partners stress that the challenge is not just to demand stronger data protection laws on paper, but to ensure that communities themselves have the digital literacy and civic skills needed to defend their rights, combat disinformation, and hold states and corporations accountable for abuses of power. Recent examples of internet shutdowns—from Myanmar's blackout to targeted regional restrictions in Nigeria and Sudan—show how quickly connectivity can be weaponized to silence opposition, dismantle movements, and hide abuses from global scrutiny. At the same time, major social media platforms have faced mounting criticism for failing to prevent hate speech, algorithmic bias, and the spread of fake news that undermines democratic discourse.

DRIF's message is clear: protecting digital civic space must be proactive, collective, and rooted in local contexts. It demands that governments commit to transparent lawmaking and respect for international human rights norms, that companies build privacy safeguards into their platforms and resist state pressure to enable censorship or intrusive data collection, and that civil society continue to build coalitions that empower ordinary people to speak up without fear of retribution. The forum's emphasis on Digital Ubuntu recognizes that technological solutions alone are not enough; cultural values of care, mutual responsibility, and inclusive dialogue must shape how Africa's digital future is governed.

By bringing together activists, researchers, grassroots organizers, policymakers, and the private sector, DRIF exemplifies what a collaborative, people-centered approach to digital rights can look like in practice. The conversations held there are increasingly relevant far beyond Africa, offering inspiration for global debates about how to defend freedom of expression, tackle digital authoritarianism, and build truly inclusive digital economies. As 'Gbenga Sesan warned, "When I see 'national security' in any policy, I'm going to question it"—a reminder that critical thinking, vigilance, and shared action are vital if the internet is to remain a space where democracy not only survives but expands. The stakes are high: in a world where shrinking offline civic space is a reality for millions, the integrity and openness of the digital realm may well determine the future of democratic participation itself.

➔ Key Insights

- Africa faces accelerated shrinking of civic space; digital space emerges as the final frontier for free expression and civic action.
- Overly permissive national security laws and internet shutdowns pose serious threats to digital freedoms.
- Framing policy through Digital Ubuntu centers African communal values in designing digital environments that are inclusive, respectful, and collectively accountable.
- Multi-stakeholder platforms like DRIF are vital for cross-sector policy innovation, blending cultural authenticity with global best practices.
- Collaboration with local networks (e.g., Bloggers of Zambia, Internews) ensures that policies remain charitably aligned with community realities and lived experiences.

Discussion Questions

1. How does digitalisation both expand and restrict civic space?
2. What are the main risks posed by surveillance technologies for civil society actors?
3. Why is internet shutdown a powerful tool for authoritarian regimes?
4. How can civil society address the challenges of algorithmic bias and opaque content moderation?
5. What examples show that digital literacy is essential for civic empowerment?
6. How do data protection frameworks like the GDPR influence global digital rights debates?
7. What should be the responsibilities of technology companies in protecting civic space?

Key Terms and Concepts

Civic Space – The physical and digital environments in which people exercise freedom of association, expression, and assembly.

Digital Rights – Fundamental human rights that ensure individuals can access, use, create, and share digital media and information safely.

Surveillance Capitalism – The commodification of personal data by private companies for profit and influence.

Internet Shutdowns – State-imposed restrictions cutting off internet access to suppress dissent or control information.

Algorithmic Governance – The use of automated systems to moderate, rank, or prioritize digital content.

Digital Divide – The gap between those with adequate access to digital tools and connectivity and those without.

Biometric Surveillance – Monitoring individuals using physical traits like fingerprints or facial recognition.

Encryption – Technology that secures communication to protect privacy.

GDPR (General Data Protection Regulation) – The EU's data privacy law that sets global standards for personal data protection.

Digital Literacy – The skills needed to navigate, evaluate, and create information in digital spaces.

Reference

Brot für die Welt. (2022). *Digitalisation and Civic Space: Threats and Opportunities.* Brot für die Welt Policy Paper.

Learning Objectives

By the end of this chapter, students will be able to:

- Explain the key challenges and opportunities facing NGOs and CBOs in the current global context.
- Analyze why flexible, core funding is vital for the sustainability of grassroots organizations.
- Describe the role of trust-based partnerships in strengthening global civil society.
- Evaluate the importance of participatory monitoring and learning frameworks.
- Discuss how digital threats and innovations shape the future of civil society organizing.
- Reflect on the significance of investing in invisible infrastructure and intergenerational leadership for NGO resilience.

Civil Society at a Turning Point

In an era defined by cascading global challenges—from authoritarian crackdowns to climate collapse, refugee crises to pandemics—the resilience and adaptability of NGOs and community-based organizations (CBOs) will determine whether global civil society survives and thrives in the decades ahead. As highlighted by the Global Fund for Community Foundations in "Strengthening civil society: The unseen battle for the future of NGOs and CBOs," today's civil society faces mounting pressures on multiple fronts: shrinking civic space, stricter regulations, rising populism and nationalism, and a funding landscape that is becoming increasingly constrained and competitive. For the next generation of global civil society actors, this is both a moment of crisis and a critical window of opportunity to redefine how civil society is built, funded, and sustained.

One of the most urgent directions for the future is fundamentally rethinking how civil society is financed. Traditional models have too often created dependency traps: funders dictate narrow project deliverables and rigid timelines, while local organizations struggle to secure core funds for staff salaries, office costs, or capacity development. Many organizations spend disproportionate time chasing short-term project grants instead of investing in their own growth and sustainability. This undermines local ownership and long-term impact. More leaders are now calling for a decisive shift toward flexible, long-term core support—funding that can be adapted to local priorities, changing contexts, and the unpredictable crises that communities face. Flexible capital enables organizations to retain experienced staff, experiment with new approaches, and pivot rapidly when crises hit. As one local grantee noted, "When you have core funds, you have room to breathe, to plan ahead, and to stand firm for your community's priorities instead of chasing donor trends."

Toward Resilient and Equitable Civil Society Structures

But funding reform alone is not enough. It must go hand in hand with internal strengthening and a radical shift in accountability systems. Many NGOs and CBOs are still forced to devote huge amounts of energy to burdensome donor reporting cycles. Monitoring, Evaluation, and Learning (MEL) frameworks too often remain extractive: they collect data to satisfy donor requirements rather than empowering communities to learn and adapt together. The future must move toward participatory MEL, where communities themselves co-design what success means, co-generate evidence, and use data as a tool for local decision-making. This approach transforms accountability from a one-way flow upward to donors into a two-way process that centers the community's agency.

Administrative burdens must be tackled too. Many small organizations are overwhelmed by redundant paperwork, complex forms, and rigid reporting templates that duplicate effort and divert precious capacity away from field work. Some progressive funders are experimenting with streamlined processes—accepting local language reports, flexible formats like short reflections instead of standard logframes, and multi-year agreements that reduce the endless cycle of re-application. This evolution must become the norm, not the exception, if local civil society is to regain time and energy for mission-driven work.

Another defining priority is the renewal of trust-based partnerships between donors, international NGOs, and grassroots CBOs. Too often, funding relationships feel top-down and transactional, with grantees treated as service providers rather than equal partners. This undermines collaboration, stifles innovation, and perpetuates power imbalances. New models call for co-creation, where communities shape grant priorities from the outset, co-design implementation plans, and share responsibility for defining outcomes and evaluating impact. Donors and INGOs must accept that true partnership involves shifting some power—moving from policing compliance to nurturing genuine collaboration. Where this happens, trust grows and outcomes are more likely to reflect what communities actually need.

To make this possible at scale, the philanthropic sector must also invest in collaborative infrastructure. Foundations and bilateral funders need to harmonize grant systems, align reporting requirements, and share due diligence processes. Doing so reduces duplication, cuts transaction costs, and allows more money and energy to flow directly to frontline work. These shifts can also unlock collective action—enabling funders to pool resources, coordinate strategies, and sustain bold, long-term responses to systemic challenges like climate change, gender justice, or democratic decline.

A further priority is strengthening the invisible but essential infrastructure that keeps civil society healthy: governance structures, financial management systems, leadership development, digital security, and community accountability mechanisms. These often go underfunded because they are "unseen"—harder to measure than the number of workshops run or reports delivered. Yet without this infrastructure, NGOs and CBOs are brittle: vulnerable to leadership turnover, donor withdrawal, political attacks, or cyber threats. Investing in these foundations builds resilience and makes organizations more capable of weathering crises, adapting to change, and delivering impact sustainably.

Reimagining Power and Participation in Civil Society

Innovation will also play a crucial role in shaping the future of global civil society. Many organizations feel the tension between remaining true to mission and the constant push to scale up, diversify revenue, or align with donor branding priorities. To resist the risk of mission drift, organizations must recommit to ethical branding, transparent governance, and open dialogue with the communities they serve. Internal democracy—creating ways for staff, volunteers, and local stakeholders to shape strategic choices—is emerging as a vital source of legitimacy. Younger activists increasingly demand horizontal, participatory leadership models over rigid hierarchies.

The digital era, while enabling new forms of organizing, also brings rising threats. NGOs must develop digital security literacy to defend against surveillance, hacking, and online harassment. Collaboration with civic tech communities and ethical technologists will be key in defending free civic space in a world where information flows can be manipulated or weaponized.

Finally, civil society must nurture the next generation of leaders who can bridge local knowledge and global solidarity. This means investing in young people's leadership, fostering intergenerational learning, and ensuring that diverse voices—women, Indigenous communities, LGBTQ+ activists, people with disabilities—are not just beneficiaries but co-leaders of global civil society agendas.

In the end, the unseen battle for the future of NGOs and global civil society is not just about money or institutional design. It is about defending the fundamental right of people everywhere to come together, organize freely, challenge injustice, and shape the rules that govern their lives. If this right erodes, so does our collective capacity to solve the world's greatest crises—from climate chaos to rising inequality, from democratic erosion to the backlash against human rights.

The stakes are clear: if civil society organizations can adapt with courage, equity, and trust at their core, they will remain one of the world's strongest counterweights to unchecked power and the complacency of the status quo. They will remind us that the real power lies not only in capital or government, but in the unstoppable conviction that ordinary people, when organized and resourced, can change everything.

Related Article to Read:

Funds for NGOs. (n.d.). The impact of NGO participation in UN General Assembly sessions. Retrieved from https://www2.fundsforngos.org/articles/the-impact-of-ngo-participation-in-un-general-assembly-sessions/

Key Summary

NGO participation in the United Nations General Assembly (UNGA) has evolved significantly over recent decades, transforming these organizations from passive observers into proactive contributors who shape global agendas and influence international decision-making. Their presence demonstrates the practical potential of global civil society to bridge the gap between intergovernmental processes and the everyday realities faced by people around the world.

Through accreditation, NGOs gain access to meetings, conferences, and side events where they can present independent reports, provide expert testimony, and deliver grassroots perspectives directly to diplomats and state representatives. This access allows NGOs to elevate issues that might otherwise be sidelined—such as indigenous rights, climate justice, gender equality, and human rights violations. By injecting evidence, community experiences, and moral arguments into negotiations, NGOs often help shift the narrative and expand the scope of debates at the UNGA.

Furthermore, NGOs play a critical watchdog role by tracking the promises made by governments on the global stage and monitoring whether these commitments translate into concrete action at the national or local level. Many NGOs produce shadow reports, run awareness campaigns, and launch public advocacy to keep states accountable for pledges related to sustainable development goals, climate targets, or humanitarian obligations. Their capacity to mobilize media attention and build coalitions adds extra leverage, putting reputational pressure on governments to uphold international standards.

Participation at the UNGA also opens doors for NGOs to build strategic alliances with other civil society actors, international organizations, and sympathetic governments. These informal networks often generate policy proposals, joint statements, and cross-border campaigns that influence the final wording of resolutions or shape implementation frameworks. Despite not having formal voting power, NGOs have succeeded in influencing landmark agreements—such as the inclusion of civil society language in sustainable development resolutions or gender-sensitive provisions in human rights declarations.

However, NGOs still face structural barriers. Limited funding, complex accreditation processes, and unequal access favor large, well-resourced organizations, often headquartered in the Global North. Smaller grassroots groups from the Global South still struggle to have their voices heard at the same level, which raises questions about representation and equity within civil society participation. Even so, the continued push for more inclusive accreditation rules and the expansion of virtual participation are signs that the UN system recognizes the irreplaceable value NGOs bring to global governance.

In sum, the impact of NGO participation at UNGA sessions is not only about direct influence on official negotiations but also about how these organizations transform the multilateral system into a more transparent, participatory, and accountable arena. By acting as intermediaries between local communities and global institutions, NGOs ensure that intergovernmental diplomacy remains rooted in real human needs and aspirations. This dynamic role reinforces the democratic legitimacy of the UN as a space for collective problem-solving beyond the narrow interests of states alone.

➔ Key Insights

- Influence without votes: NGOs prove that you don't need a seat at the voting table to impact policy outcomes when you have credibility, networks, and public voice.
- Bridging local-global gaps: Their ability to translate local community needs into global discussions makes UNGA sessions more connected to everyday realities.
- Watchdog function: NGOs sustain pressure for accountability after states make promises in New York—an essential check in the global governance system.

Discussion Questions

1. Why do many civil society leaders argue that traditional donor funding models need to change? Give examples of how flexible core funding could make a difference in practice.
2. What are the risks and benefits of closer partnerships between donors, international NGOs, and local community-based organizations?
3. How can participatory Monitoring, Evaluation, and Learning (MEL) empower local communities instead of simply satisfying donor requirements?
4. In an era of digital surveillance and online repression, what strategies should NGOs adopt to protect civic space and secure digital infrastructure?
5. What does "invisible infrastructure" mean in the context of civil society, and why is it so critical for long-term resilience?
6. How can civil society ensure that younger, diverse leaders play meaningful roles in shaping the future of global activism?

Key Terms and Concepts

Core Funding – Unrestricted financial support that organizations can allocate flexibly to strengthen capacity and respond to local priorities.

Participatory MEL (Monitoring, Evaluation, and Learning) – An approach that involves communities in defining success and using data to inform collective learning.

Trust-Based Philanthropy – Funding relationships built on transparency, mutual accountability, and co-creation, rather than rigid compliance checks.

Invisible Infrastructure – Organizational foundations like governance systems, staff training, financial management, and digital security that sustain an NGO's operations.

Digital Civic Space – The online environment in which civil society actors organize, communicate, and advocate— often contested by surveillance and misinformation.

Mission Drift – The risk that an organization loses its core purpose by aligning too closely with donor trends or external branding pressures.

Intergenerational Leadership – Ensuring the transfer of knowledge and power to emerging leaders, especially marginalized youth and underrepresented groups.

Reference

Global Fund for Community Foundations. (2022). Strengthening civil society: The unseen battle for the future of NGOs and CBOs.

Learning Objectives

By the end of this chapter, students will be able to:

- Identify major global NGO campaigns that have influenced international law, policy, or corporate behavior.
- Analyze the strategies and coalitions that made these campaigns successful.
- Evaluate how local communities and transnational networks interacted in each case.
- Reflect on the limitations, criticisms, and lessons learned from these real-world campaigns.

Civil Society as a Driving Force in Global Transformation

Across history, some of the most transformative changes in global governance, human rights, and sustainability have not come solely from states or corporations but from the collective efforts of ordinary people—organized through NGOs, grassroots alliances, and transnational networks. These campaigns remind us that global civil society is not an abstract idea but a living force, driven by concrete actions that challenge injustice, hold power to account, and expand what we believe is possible.

Landmark Civil Society Campaigns and Their Global Impact

One powerful example is the International Campaign to Ban Landmines (ICBL), which began as a coalition of small organizations and grew into a global movement that successfully pressured states to adopt the 1997 Mine Ban Treaty. The ICBL's grassroots-driven approach mobilized survivors, medical workers, and local deminers to testify before diplomats, turning abstract statistics into human stories that governments could not ignore. By 2023, more than 160 countries had signed the treaty, and global landmine casualties have dropped by more than half compared to the early 1990s—a testament to how sustained civil society pressure can change international norms.

Equally instructive is the role NGOs played in the creation of the International Criminal Court (ICC). Throughout the 1990s, the Coalition for the International Criminal Court (CICC)—an alliance of over 2,500 civil society groups worldwide—lobbied governments to ensure that the Rome Statute included robust human rights protections. This grassroots diplomacy helped enshrine the principle that certain crimes, like genocide and war crimes, transcend national sovereignty. Though the ICC still faces political pushback, its very existence owes much to persistent, networked

NGO advocacy that refused to accept impunity as inevitable.

At the intersection of corporate accountability and civil society activism, the Bangladesh Accord on Fire and Building Safety stands as a sobering yet hopeful story. In 2013, the Rana Plaza garment factory collapse killed over 1,100 workers and injured thousands more—one of the deadliest industrial disasters in history. Within weeks, global labor unions and NGOs like the Clean Clothes Campaign and Worker Rights Consortium coordinated international outrage into binding commitments. Major apparel brands were compelled to sign the Accord, which mandated independent inspections and legal obligations to fix safety hazards. By 2022, more than 1,600 factories had been covered, improving working conditions for over 2.5 million workers. This case underscores that global supply chains are not "too big to change" when NGOs align local workers' voices with global consumer pressure, real accountability is possible.

Environmental campaigns also show how local struggles ripple globally. The Stop the Keystone XL Pipeline campaign in North America combined Indigenous leadership, local landowners, climate scientists, and NGOs like 350.org to halt a massive fossil fuel infrastructure project. After a decade of legal battles and grassroots mobilization, the project was officially canceled in 2021. The victory demonstrated that community-led resistance, amplified by digital organizing and media strategies, can rewrite what was once dismissed as inevitable economic development.

Digital Rights and the Expanding Civic Frontier

Beyond climate, the global push for digital rights is reshaping civil society's frontier. Organizations such as Access Now, the Electronic Frontier Foundation, and Privacy International are fighting to protect privacy, freedom of expression, and online civic space. They challenge mass surveillance, advocate for strong data protection laws like the EU's General Data Protection Regulation (GDPR), and expose abuses of biometric systems. Strategic litigation in India, for example, secured a landmark Supreme Court ruling that privacy is a fundamental right—shaping debates far beyond its borders. In Kenya, civil society coalitions have pushed for oversight of the Huduma Namba digital ID system, highlighting risks of exclusion and data misuse.

The threat landscape continues to evolve with the rise of artificial intelligence. In 2023, more than 150 NGOs from 40+ countries joined the Global Campaign for AI Accountability, pushing for transparent, human rights–centered governance of AI systems. They demand independent audits, explainable algorithms, and protections for vulnerable communities against algorithmic bias—especially in contexts like predictive policing or social welfare systems. By connecting lawyers, technologists, and community advocates, this movement insists that AI must serve the public good, not deepen inequality or erode civic freedoms.

Community-Rooted Solutions and Participatory Models

Equally important are campaigns that rarely make international headlines but transform lives locally. Community foundations worldwide, such as the Southern Africa Trust or the Global Fund for Community Foundations, build platforms for local leaders to decide funding priorities. They champion flexible, core funding so that communities can define what development means for them—whether that is food sovereignty, local schools, or renewable energy projects. This "local first" model challenges traditional donor-driven agendas and shows that sustainable change must be rooted in trust-based, community-led solutions.

These stories illustrate a vital lesson: meaningful campaigns blend insider strategy with outsider pressure, global networks with local realities, and principled confrontation with practical partnerships. NGOs succeed when they adapt to shifting contexts—investing in digital security to resist surveillance, using big data and satellite imagery to track deforestation, or building alliances with ethical businesses to drive systemic change.

Yet success brings its own tensions. The same campaigns that win global recognition must guard against mission drift, donor dependency, or co-optation by corporate greenwashing. Many NGOs now experiment with participatory governance, transparent funding models, and ethical branding to sustain credibility. Younger movements, in particular, demand flatter hierarchies and open, inclusive leadership that reflects the diversity of the communities they serve.

Lessons and the Path Forward for Global Civil Society

The stakes have never been higher. The climate emergency demands rapid decarbonization that disrupts entrenched industries. The struggle for digital rights pits civil society against surveillance states and powerful tech monopolies. Rising authoritarianism shrinks civic space, while disinformation and algorithmic manipulation threaten the very idea of informed public debate.

In this turbulent context, global NGO campaigns remain a source of hope and a laboratory of democratic resilience. They remind us that no injustice is too entrenched to be challenged, no institution too powerful to be held accountable. They show that solidarity can cross borders faster than capital, that grassroots knowledge can confront elite narratives, and that ordinary people, when connected, can co-create extraordinary solutions.

For students of global civil society, these campaigns offer more than stories—they are living blueprints. They teach how to align moral vision with practical strategy, how to build alliances across difference, and how to sustain collective action in the face of backlash or fatigue. They prove that global governance is not just about treaties and summits but about the patient, risky, often imperfect work of countless communities who refuse to settle for the world as it is.

In the end, the future of global civil society will not be written solely by states or corporations but by those who dare to organize, to speak truth to power, and to imagine—again and again—a more just, democratic, and sustainable world for all.

Related Article to Read:

Funds for NGOs. (n.d.). The 10 best fundraising campaigns that changed the NGO sector. Funds for NGOs. Retrieved from https://www2.fundsforngos.org/articles-searching-grants-and-donors/the-10-best-fundraising-campaigns-that-changed-the-ngo-sector/

➔ Key Summary

This article highlights ten groundbreaking fundraising campaigns that have reshaped the NGO and nonprofit fundraising landscape through creativity, digital innovation, and community-driven engagement. Each campaign serves as a compelling example of how NGOs have moved beyond traditional donor appeals to adopt storytelling, peer-to-peer networks, and smart use of technology to mobilize global support.

The Red Cross, for instance, has consistently demonstrated how large-scale emergency fundraising can quickly gather resources from millions of individual donors to deliver rapid humanitarian aid during crises such as earthquakes, tsunamis, or conflicts. Similarly, UNICEF has mastered the use of emotive storytelling and viral video campaigns to spotlight urgent issues like child poverty, vaccination, and education, converting global attention into sustained donations.

One of the most iconic digital examples is the ALS Ice Bucket Challenge, which went viral in 2014 and raised over $200 million for ALS research. It showed the world the power of social media driven, user-generated content to break fundraising records without large budgets or traditional advertising. Another innovative model is ShareTheMeal, an award-winning app developed by the UN World Food Programme that allows individuals to donate the cost of a meal with a single tap—turning micro-donations into over 200 million meals for people in need.

During the COVID-19 pandemic, the Run for Heroes campaign in the UK showed how simple, peer-to-peer digital challenges could tap into people's desire to contribute while staying connected during lockdowns. The campaign's structure—run 5K, donate £5, and nominate 5 friends—raised over £7 million for NHS charities, all while spreading through personal networks instead of traditional fundraising channels.

The Big Give Christmas Challenge demonstrates how matching funds and deadlines can motivate people to give more by doubling their impact. This annual campaign has become the UK's biggest online match funding event, bringing together charities, philanthropists, and corporate partners to amplify donations.

These campaigns share common elements: powerful narratives that resonate emotionally, easy participation mechanisms that lower barriers to entry, the use of real-time updates and transparent impact tracking, and smart integration of digital platforms to reach people where they already are—on their phones and social media feeds.

Another critical takeaway is that successful campaigns focus not just on raising money once, but on building long-term relationships with supporters. By transforming donors into advocates and community members, these campaigns help NGOs grow networks of people who stay engaged, share causes with their own networks, and provide sustained support.

Together, these ten case studies illustrate how the NGO sector is innovating to adapt to changing donor expectations, digital disruption, and global challenges. They also show that memorable fundraising doesn't rely on massive marketing budgets alone, but on bold ideas, authentic stories, and genuine community spirit.

Ultimately, this article provides inspiration and practical insights for NGOs looking to design campaigns that go beyond transactions to build trust, activate communities, and deliver measurable impact in ways that strengthen the organization's mission for the long term.

➔ Key Insights

- Emotional storytelling and user-generated content drive virality, as seen with the Ice Bucket Challenge raising over $220 million
- Peer challenges (e.g. "donate $5, nominate 5") and matching campaigns create social pressure and boost participation.
- микrotargeted digital tools, such as smartphone apps and online donation platforms, enable frictionless giving and real-time engagement.
- Campaigns linked to global events (like COVID-19 or humanitarian crises) have the power to mobilize mass support quickly.
- Structurally creative models—like ShareTheMeal (meals for clicks) and Big Give's Christmas Challenge (match funding)—merge innovation with measurable impact.

Discussion Questions

1. How did the International Campaign to Ban Landmines demonstrate the impact of grassroots pressure on international law?
2. In what ways did the Bangladesh Accord change global supply chain accountability after the Rana Plaza disaster?
3. Why is flexible core funding critical for local campaigns to succeed in global civil society?
4. How do digital rights campaigns challenge surveillance capitalism and protect civic space online?
5. What do these global campaigns teach us about balancing insider advocacy with grassroots mobilization?

Key Terms and Concepts

International Criminal Court (ICC) – A permanent international tribunal created partly through NGO advocacy to prosecute crimes against humanity, genocide, and war crimes.

Bangladesh Accord – A legally binding agreement between global brands and trade unions/NGOs to improve factory safety after the Rana Plaza collapse.

Supply Chain Accountability – The practice of holding corporations responsible for labor, environmental, and human rights conditions across their global production networks.

Surveillance Capitalism – The business model where companies collect and monetize massive amounts of personal data.

Algorithmic Bias – Systemic discrimination that occurs when AI or algorithms reproduce or amplify unfair social patterns.

Digital Rights – Fundamental rights that protect freedom of expression, privacy, and access to information online.

Flexible Core Funding – Unrestricted funding that allows local organizations to cover staff, governance, and emergent needs beyond project-specific budgets.

Social License to Operate – Informal public approval that companies need to maintain legitimacy in the communities where they work.

Grassroots Mobilization – Collective action led by local communities to advocate for change.

Transnational Advocacy Networks (TANs) – Networks linking NGOs, activists, and local groups across borders to tackle global issues.

Mission Drift – When an organization shifts away from its original purpose due to external pressures, such as donor or corporate influence.

Ethical Branding – Strategies NGOs use to maintain credibility and transparency while communicating their mission.

Trust-Based Partnerships – Collaborative relationships built on mutual accountability, co-creation, and respect for local leadership.

Chapter 12. Conclusion

As we reach the end of this exploration of NGOs and Global Civil Society, one truth becomes clear: civil society is not a fixed institution but a living, contested, and evolving practice. From the earliest voluntary associations that challenged the slave trade or demanded women's suffrage, to today's digital movements fighting climate inaction or surveillance capitalism, civil society has always been a force that insists another world is possible—and that ordinary people have the right and the power to shape it.

This book has shown that NGOs occupy an unusual and sometimes uncomfortable position in global governance. They are insiders and outsiders at once—lobbyists in the corridors of the United Nations, watchdogs exposing hidden abuses, trusted partners in community development, and sometimes radical disruptors confronting entrenched power. They are praised for filling gaps where states fail and markets exploit, yet they are also scrutinized for being unelected, dependent on donor agendas, or vulnerable to co-optation.

Such contradictions are not flaws to be erased but tensions to be managed with honesty, courage, and commitment to democratic principles. Civil society's legitimacy has always rested not on formal authority but on the moral force of collective action, transparent governance, and deep accountability to the people and communities it claims to serve. In an age of shrinking civic space, rising disinformation, and new digital frontiers of surveillance, this legitimacy must be defended—and renewed—through constant adaptation and self-reflection.

Throughout this course, you have traced the arc of NGOs from local charities to global policy actors. You have analyzed their role in shaping international law, building cross-sector partnerships, and navigating the dilemmas of professionalization, branding, and insider–outsider dynamics. You have explored how technology can both empower marginalized voices and amplify repression. You have debated how funding structures, participatory learning, and intergenerational leadership can help or hinder civil society's mission.

And, crucially, you have asked what it means for NGOs to contribute not just to service delivery but to systemic transformation—holding governments accountable, challenging corporate abuses, and standing up for the rights of those whose voices are often silenced.

These lessons matter because the stakes could not be higher. We live in an era defined by intertwined crises: a climate emergency that transcends borders; waves of forced displacement that test our compassion and our institutions; pandemics that reveal both our interdependence and our inequality; the rise of authoritarianism and shrinking civic spaces in places where democracy was once taken for granted. In this context, the question is not whether civil society is relevant—but whether it can adapt quickly enough, stay true enough to its principles, and organize broadly enough to meet challenges that no single actor can solve alone.

The chapters of this book argue that the future of global civil society rests on three interconnected commitments:

1. A commitment to trust and solidarity: True partnerships—between funders and grassroots actors, between international NGOs and local communities—must be built on humility, co-creation, and shared power. When civil society loses trust, it loses its reason for being.

2. A commitment to resilience and innovation: From digital security to participatory governance, from flexible core funding to new models of leadership, NGOs must

invest in the "invisible infrastructure" that allows them to survive shocks, withstand political pressure, and adapt to fast-changing contexts.

3. A commitment to critical hope: Civil society cannot afford complacency, nor should it abandon its role as a radical challenger of the status quo. Even while engaging states and corporations in pragmatic cooperation, civil society must preserve spaces for dissent, imagination, and transformation.

As students, future researchers, practitioners, or simply global citizens, you now stand at the edge of these debates. The knowledge you have gained is not an end but an invitation—to ask deeper questions, to scrutinize claims of legitimacy and impact, and to find your own place in the networks and movements that connect local action to global change.

Whether you choose to work for an NGO, shape policy as a public servant, create ethical businesses, or support your community through grassroots organizing, remember that the real power of global civil society lies not in its institutions alone but in its people: the teachers, youth leaders, activists, journalists, volunteers, and everyday citizens who refuse to accept injustice as inevitable.

As the Global Fund for Community Foundations reminds us, "Civil society is an ecosystem that depends on trust, solidarity, and sustained care." To protect this ecosystem is to protect our shared capacity to face the defining challenges of our century—and to imagine a future in which justice, dignity, and freedom remain not abstract ideals but lived realities.

May this book give you the tools to see the world more clearly, the courage to question it more deeply, and the inspiration to change it more boldly.

Thank you for learning, reflecting, and imagining together. The work continues—beyond these pages, and with you.

Dong-uk Kim

Dong-uk Kim earned his Bachelor's degree in Humanities and International Studies from Pusan National University, followed by a Master's and Ph.D. in International Studies from the Graduate School of International Studies at the same university. Inspired by a 2023 meeting with Nobel Peace Prize laureate Muhammad Yunus, he founded Yunus Korea, a non-profit organization, in 2024 and serves as its founding Chairperson. He is actively building domestic and international partnerships to expand the social business ecosystem. Additionally, since 2024, he has been an adjunct professor at Pusan National University's Graduate School of International Studies, working to bridge academic theory with practical application in social economy and international development cooperation.

NGOs and Global Civil Society

초판 인쇄 2025년 8월 22일
초판 발행 2025년 8월 29일

저　자 김동욱

디자인·편집 배영미
발행인 최재원
펴낸곳 부산대학교출판문화원

출판등록 제1983-000001호 1983.11.10.
부산광역시 금정구 부산대학로 63번길 2 (우편번호46241)
대표전화 051-510-1932 팩시밀리 051-512-7812
https://press.pusan.ac.kr

※ 이 도서는 부산대학교출판문화원의 강의교재 개발 지원사업(2025-2)지원으로 제작되었습니다.

ISBN 978 - 89 - 7316 - 842 - 2 (93300)